WAKE UP
YOU COULD LOSE YOUR TEEN TO SUICIDE:

A Father's Guide to Dealing with Teenage Depression & Anxiety

Chris Coulter

Copyright © 2023

All Rights Reserved

ISBN:

979-8-9896304-3-1

Dedication

These words are dedicated to my three pillars of strength—my eternal inspiration—Maddie, Zac, and Sawyer.

Maddie, your strength of character and the sacrifices you made to uplift the underdog resonate deeply within our hearts. Your acknowledgment that our sometimes-challenging relationship was rooted in our similarities remains the highest compliment. The void left by your passing is immense, yet your message has become a lifeline for countless families, inspiring mental health initiatives. The milestones we could have shared are dearly missed, but your legacy lives on in the hearts of those you touched. As I encounter your friends, they express how much you are missed every day. My only regret is that they cannot tell you in person. You are my True North.

Zac and Sawyer, your young lives have endured more heartache than deserved. Yet, you both stand as beacons of bravery, compassion, and leadership. Your messages have touched the lives of many, making a heroic difference in the world. You do it not for accolades but as a tribute to your fallen sister, hoping to spare other children the pain you've encountered. Your strength has transformed me into a better person, and I eagerly anticipate the greatness that unfolds on your paths. You both make me immensely proud.

This book is also dedicated to all the families facing struggles today and in the future. Today may echo with challenges, but tomorrow's melody will harmonize with the resilience of love, crafting a lifetime of triumph over adversity. Remember, this too shall pass. Share your story when you emerge on the other side of your ordeal. Hope is a precious commodity we all need more of in this world. You will overcome, and the journey will leave you stronger, wiser, and a better parent.

To all parents and future parents, here are a few nuggets of wisdom. Parenting is a remarkable yet challenging adventure. Embrace the boundless curiosity of your little ones and encourage them to take risks. Let them learn from the inevitable mistakes, for those lessons are the building blocks of wisdom. Don't shy away from tough conversations. Dive into the depths of their thoughts, push through the discomfort, and truly understand what's on their minds. Create an environment where every topic is fair game. Make it known that no conversation is off-limits. This openness fosters trust—a two-way street where you learn to trust them as they trust you. Remember, you're not the enemy, even though there might be moments when they make you feel like one.

Parenting is an ongoing journey filled with highs and lows. Embrace it, savour the precious moments, and navigate the challenges with patience and love. You're not just raising children but nurturing future leaders, dreamers, and compassionate individuals. So, embark on this adventure with an open heart, and remember, the rewards far outweigh the challenges.

Chris Coulter

Acknowledgment

Writing a book is a big undertaking. I had no idea what I was getting myself into when I started. My journey of gratitude started well before I sat down to write my first sentence.

My boys, Zac and Sawyer, continue to provide the strength and support needed to face the world, even on its most challenging days.

Mom and Dad, you've stood by me throughout this entire process, despite not always fully understanding the depth of my journey. You, too, lost your granddaughter too early, and I know the ache of missing her daily.

To Jen: You've been my rock and my most fervent cheerleader. Your unwavering presence beside me on this rollercoaster ride speaks volumes, and I'm grateful you never attempted to disembark from the journey.

To Kadeem: Your words mean so much to our family. Know that Maddie adored you. You are making such an incredible difference in the lives of young adults. You and Marina will be amazing parents.

Special thanks to those who had my back throughout this ordeal: Jaime & Leslie, Michael & Norine, Don, Rosie, Billy, Geoff & Nancy, Melanie Rousseau, Mark Halpern, Jim Ruta, Caroline, Nikki, Kristi, Bob Calvert, Dr. G, Reddog, the staff of 7 North at NYGH and many others too numerous to mention.

To Nicole: Despite the unimaginable loss of our daughter, you continue to do incredible things in Maddie's name with The Maddie Project. Our shared angel and two incredible boys are reasons for eternal gratitude.

To everyone who supported my writing and encouraged me to embark on this adventure at a new level, I appreciate your unwavering belief. I hope it was worth the wait.

To the parents who reached out, sharing the struggles with their young adults, you are the true reason behind this book. May your family find a happy ending, and always remember, you are not alone.

Lastly, to my angel and first unconditional love, Maddie. Without you, none of this would be possible. You will always be my inspiration and guiding light. I have lots more to do in life before I join you. Together, we will make this world a better place. I'm grateful to feel you beside me on this journey.

Contents

Dedication iv

Acknowledgment vi

About the Author xii

Forward xiv

Preface xvi

Introduction April 10, 2015 1

Module 1 The Perfect Child 6

Chapter 1: It Started Like a Fairy Tale 7

Chapter 2: The Loneliness Epidemic: The Silent 12

Module 2: The Signs 17

Chapter 3: Our Actions Have Consequences 18

Chapter 4: New Location, Same Situation 23

Chapter 5: The White Elephant Gets Liberated 26

Chapter 6: There's No Such Thing as a Good 30

Chapter 7: Navigating the Emotional Roller 33

Chapter 8: Balancing Act: Navigating Finances 38

Chapter 9: When School Becomes a Burden 41

Chapter 10: The First Attempt or a Cry for Help? 44

Chapter 11 Our Home on 7 North 49

Chapter 13: The Return to 7 North 57

Module 3: The Lessons 65

Chapter 13: A Father's Path to Understanding 66

Chapter 14: What is it Like for a Parent Whose 69

Chapter 15: Does the Sadness Ever Stop? 73

Module 4: The Factors 77

Chapter 16: Social Media: The High Price of Likes ... 78

Chapter 17: Navigating the Teenage Years: 82

Chapter 18: Navigating Divorce: Creating a 88

Chapter 19: Igniting Your Child's Passion: The 90

Chapter 20: Unveiling the Hidden Struggles: 92

Chapter 21: Navigating a Journey of Trust 95

Chapter 22: Embarking on the Journey to 98

Chapter 23: The Pressures of Being a Teenager 101

Module 5: The Future 104

Chapter 24: Prevention Versus Remediation? 105

Chapter 25: Greater Emphasis on Teaching 110

Chapter 26: To Be an Activist or Not? 114

Chapter 27: Creating Resources for Parents 116

Chapter 28: What Are Your 13 Reasons to Thrive? .. 118

Module 6: The Reflection 122

Chapter 29: Time Gives Us the Ability to Reflect 123

Chapter 30: How Children Navigate the Sudden 128

Chapter 31: From Siblings to Pillars: The Impact....131

Chapter 32: How I Will Choose to Remember..........135

Chapter 33: Embracing Resilience: Illuminating ... 139

Module 7: Mental Health Resources.........................142

Purpose of this Section: 143

    Example Entry: 144

    Emergency & Mental Health Facilities 146

    Sources: 149

About the Author

Chris Coulter is not your typical entrepreneur; he's a dynamic force with a flair for both business and storytelling. Boasting three thrilling decades as a serial entrepreneur across diverse industries, Coulter's journey takes a riveting turn with a fervent commitment to writing and mental health advocacy.

In the crucible of personal tragedy, the heart-wrenching loss of his 14-year-old daughter, Maddie. Coulter emerged as a dedicated parent and a passionate advocate for mental health. A maverick with a mission, he delves into the profound impact of mental illness on families, infusing his writing with an authenticity born from lived experiences.

Coulter's not-for-profit venture, focused on kids' emotional health, bears witness to his unwavering dedication. Today, he serves as a guiding force, emphasizing the crucial role of prevention in shaping teenagers' emotional resilience. Coulter is on a mission to revolutionize the dialogue around emotional health in schools and influence government policymakers to prioritize this often-overlooked aspect of education.

Beyond the pages of "Wake Up," Coulter's voice echoes through prestigious publications such as the Globe & Mail and Huffington Post. A captivating keynote speaker at Mental Health and Entrepreneur conferences, he seamlessly weaves his entrepreneurial acumen with a profound understanding of mental wellness.

When not penning compelling narratives, Coulter immerses himself in a whirlwind of activities cycling, hiking, savouring live music, and escaping to the cottage. As the founder of The Finish Line Group, he champions entrepreneurs in the realms of tax minimization, succession planning, estate planning, and strategic philanthropy, creating legacies that transcend generations.

Chris Coulter's life is woven with resilience, advocacy, and a profound love that transcends realms. He is a father to two remarkable boys, Zac and Sawyer, both thriving at the University of Guelph and Dalhousie University. And always, there's Maddie, his angel, casting a timeless gaze over his extraordinary journey.

"Wake Up; You Could Lose Your Teen to Suicide" is Coulter's first full-length published work.

Forward

By Kadeem Daley

In the ever-evolving landscape of Children's Mental Health, the commitment to understanding and addressing the unique challenges faced by today's youth should be at the forefront of today and tomorrow's agenda. As a licensed social worker, I have been dedicated to improving, educating and advocating for Children's Mental health, and I am honoured to introduce this invaluable resource and firsthand perspective from a parent.

Throughout this book, Chris delves into the journey and knowledge he and his family have built over the years, while doing everything in their powers to understand their pain and to advocate for change. The pages ahead offer more than just a guide, it is a first-hand parental experience giving you transparency into the journey of enlightenment and advocacy. I ask that you immerse yourself into the readers perspective and embrace yourself for a roller-coaster of emotions. Do not judge yourself for what you are doing today but make efforts to make tomorrow better.

My hope for you as the reader is to build knowledge, awareness and to be a part of the advocacy group for Children's Mental Health. This is not just a resource it is the next step into building a healthier more educated alliance and support for our youth today.

Kadeem Daley, MSW, RSW

Preface

Why write a book? Especially one that delves into the depths of our family's most agonizing moments. Frankly, committing these experiences to paper dragged me back through the heartache. It prompts reflection on what was done and contemplates alternative actions. Hindsight is a teacher, but its lessons find application in future mirroring the past. Parenting is no exact science; it's more akin to an art form, requiring creativity, empathy, and common sense, often responding to situations rather than anticipating them. People, especially children, defy predictability. If adults can be highly irregular, expecting children, with their evolving minds and limited life skills, to be predictable is an unrealistic standard. We can't hold them to it.

Experiences, whether positive or negative, mold us. The expectation is to be pragmatic, and self-aware, and to learn from those around us. However, many adults have yet to master life's intricacies, so why impose an expectation of perfection on kids? Should we not equip them with the tools we're still figuring out ourselves? Relying on parents alone to impart emotional intelligence, self-awareness, and self-regulation sets us up for failure. This might explain why, despite studies affirming its superiority to IQ, Emotional Intelligence (EI) levels have plateaued over the last 30 years. Schools prioritize grades over learning from mistakes. Imagine the setback if inventors, scientists, and entrepreneurs had been discouraged from making mistakes, where would society be today?

Writing this book does not claim perfection in parenting. Some might question, "You lost a daughter to suicide, so why offer parenting advice?" The claim isn't omniscience; it's a candid portrayal of parenting in its least celebrated form. Parenting is a breeze when life is predictable, and your kids aren't grappling with challenges. However, when confronted with the storm of a struggling child, the handbooks become obsolete. Few discuss the painful subjects openly. Therapists are there for that, right? The predicament in parenting lies in not always knowing how to handle our children in adversity. The best strategy is to educate ourselves and our children before the crisis hits. When they're in crisis, it's too late. Prevention is the key to addressing the growing epidemic of depressed and anxious youths.

Our schools and governments engage in finger-pointing, evading responsibility and change. Conversations with both have been attempted but pandering seems preferable to action. While many educators acknowledge the need for changes in the education curriculum, their voices need amplification. Our children's lives hinge on it.

It's effortless to highlight systemic failures, but that's not the intent of this book. This book narrates a story that could be about any child. Maddie could have been any child from any neighbourhood, province, or country. She was a popular, intelligent, wickedly funny, and empathetic young woman. When she was in turmoil, it affected those closest to her. We did everything in our power to help her, but how do you cope with a child who decides she doesn't want to live anymore?

Following Maddie's loss, writing became my coping mechanism. I had no agenda, just an innate desire to feel better. The more I wrote, the more feedback poured in from parents navigating experiences similar to ours. Many felt lost, not knowing where to turn. My writing reassured them they weren't alone in grappling with this pain. Over the years, countless messages expressing gratitude for sharing my experiences flooded in. They've kept writing, and I've kept listening. Many urged me to pen a book on the subject. I eventually heeded their advice.

My aspirations with this book are fourfold:

1) To assure other parents that they're not alone in their struggles with their teens.

2) To provide resources to parents who feel adrift when they need support the most.

3) To donate proceeds to agencies offering lifesaving services and support that are underfunded and overused.

4) To stimulate conversation on widespread changes to our education and political system.

This involves implementing proactive and preventative resources, so children comprehend the importance of identifying, understanding, and processing complex emotions.

Without these teachings, children can't be expected to navigate crises successfully. Remember, indifference has never made a difference.

Regardless of the stage you're at in parenting when you read this book, I hope my mistakes can be your lessons, leading to a happier outcome than ours. What transpired with Maddie unfolded swiftly; I hope this book imparts the understanding that suicide can happen to any family. Do not dismiss the early warning signs lightly. Most importantly, parents, awaken—your teen could be at risk of suicide.

Introduction
April 10, 2015

"The worst day becomes a chapter, not the entire story."

"Chris, Wake Up! Chris, Wake Up! Chris, Wake Up!"

That voice didn't sound right in my dream. The voice sounded like it was coming from a distance. It sounded like Caroline's voice. There was a sound of urgency, almost desperation, in her voice. The voice didn't disappear. The sound of urgency in Caroline's voice persisted as my eyes slowly opened, the transition from the disconcerting dream to the waking world marked by her desperate pleas.

Earlier that night, I had taken two Gravols and put my phone in the other room for the first time since we went down this challenging journey with Maddie's struggle. The kids weren't with me this week. I needed to sleep.

CHRIS COULTER

It had been a difficult week for me. I haven't been a great sleeper for some time. They say having kids means you've had your last great sleep for the rest of your life. The events of the last five months only added to my insomnia. Having gone through two suicide attempts by my daughter, Maddie, since December 2014 was justifiable for the lack of rest.

Like most days since December, it started on the 7th floor at North York General Hospital in the Youth & Adolescent Mental Health Unit. Nicole and I found ourselves in the familiar yet emotionally charged space, meeting with Lisa, the resident social worker in the unit. Lisa, a beacon of empathy, dedicated her days to making a profound difference in the lives of countless kids and their families residing in the unit. In the numerous sessions I shared with Lisa, her genuine care ended in tears that welled up as we navigated the turbulent waters of our struggles. However, this particular meeting surpassed the usual emotional intensity.

As the weight of the last five months bore down on me, frustration mingled with the swelling emotions, and I couldn't contain the stream of tears that broke free. The experience of being a parent to a child who questioned whether she wanted to live was a relentless emotional storm, with promising days overshadowed by countless challenging ones. Every tear shed held the weight of a thousand unspoken fears, and the vulnerability in that room was palpable. Despite our attempts at optimism, an underlying doubt lingered—a constant companion in our arduous journey, echoing through the silent sobs that punctuated the heaviness of our hearts.

Exiting the meeting with tears streaming down my face, I was met by Maddie's gaze. Attempting composure, my puffy eyes and runny nose showed my inner turmoil. Maddie, sensing my distress, approached with her trademark gentle and caring smile. At that moment, she enveloped me in a tight embrace, whispering, 'I love you, Daddy.' Her hug, normally comforting, held an unforeseen weight that I would only come to understand later.

Little did I know it would be the last time I saw Maddie.

****

"Wake up, Chris!" It was Caroline's voice. Caroline and I had been dating for the last couple of years after our marriages ended. It took me a moment to shake the effects of the Gravol I had taken a couple of hours before. I looked at my Fitbit. It was 11:39 pm on Friday, April 10th. Still dazed, I got out of bed and walked to the front door of the house I had been renting. I had inadvertently latched the chain in addition to locking the door. Now, it made sense. Caroline had a key to my house but couldn't get in because of the chain. I opened the door to see Caroline and her daughter Melissa. Both had a look of alarm and concern on their faces. I felt my heart in my stomach. I knew this wasn't good.

Caroline told me I needed to call Nicole. Nicole was my ex-wife and the mother of my three children. My 13-year-old son, Zac, had contacted Caroline because he couldn't reach me. Zac had assumed Caroline would know how to get hold of me.

I picked up my phone; I had twenty-two missed calls. A cold rush seeped through my body as I dialed Nicole. I didn't know the details, but I knew it involved Maddie. My head and heart went to a place I had feared for the past five months, but I knew it was different this time.

I got Nicole on the phone. Her voice was shaking. She explained the text she had received from Maddie an hour before. Maddie had sent a message saying she loved us and was saying goodbye. Nicole had traced her location using Find My Phone. Maddie then turned off her phone.

I had felt it earlier with the cold rush that overcame my body, but on some level, I knew we had lost her.

I told Nicole that I was coming over to her place. Zac was with her, but Sawyer had a sleepover at a friend's house.

I slowly drove over to Nicole's house. It was a 10-minute drive, but it felt a lot longer. I didn't want to face the news that was in store for me, news that I already felt the pain from. It was a surreal feeling as a wave of emotions came over me.

I turned onto Bayview Avenue; the familiar route etched into my muscle memory. The bright lights of the Granite Club, where

WAKE UP YOU COULD LOSE YOUR TEEN TO SUICIDE

Maddie had swam competitively for years, flickered in the distance. On the bridge leading to Toronto French School, where Maddie had spent her early school years until Grade 8, I passed two police cruisers with their lights flashing. The stark contrast of the vibrant lights against the darkness of the night intensified my unease. My breath quickened, and a cold sweat broke across my forehead. The sensation of nausea gripped me, almost forcing me to pull over. Just a couple of minutes away from Nicole's house, the feeling mercifully settled, allowing me to continue the sombre journey.

I pulled onto Nicole's street and saw Nicole, Zac, and my former in-laws pacing on her porch. I pulled up in front of her place and parked. I had barely stepped onto the porch when a police cruiser pulled up. The officer exited the car and slowly made his way towards us on the sidewalk. I hoped he would walk by us, but I knew his presence was intended for us. He walked toward the porch, looked down at his feet, and gently said, *"I'm sorry."*

We had lost Maddie. She was only 14 years old.

Module 1
The Perfect Child

"The moment you become a parent for the first time, you realize that your heart now beats outside your body."

Chapter 1: It Started Like a Fairy Tale

On June 28, 2000, a profound chapter in our life story unfolded as Maddie entered our world, bringing with her the indescribable joy that accompanies the birth of a child. This was more than a moment; it was my first taste of unconditional love.

In the delivery room of North York General Hospital, the morning sunlight painted a warm backdrop as Maddie made her grand entrance, marking the commencement of our journey into parenthood. Maddie's entrance into the world was marked by an excitement that resonated through the room after a day and a half of labour. Every parent would agree—nothing readies you for the visceral experience of witnessing your first child's birth. It's a moment painted with the scent of antiseptic, the warmth of the morning sun, and the echo of excitement that resonates through the room.

Parents often share narratives about the transformative power of having a child, painting vivid pictures of its impact on their lives. However, until you lock eyes with your child for the first time, those tales remain abstract, words unable to capture the depth of the emotions that surge through you.

My task on that day was clear and singular: ensuring Nicole received the relief of an epidural. In the preceding days, we had made a couple of trips to the hospital, only to be sent back home with Braxton Hicks contractions. But this particular visit proved to be different, as Maddie's life commenced much like the way she would go on to live it—on her terms.

Determination was woven into Maddie's essence from the start. Once she set her mind on something, an unwavering commitment emerged—a trait that would define her character. Dr. Browne, the deliverer of all three of our children, welcomed Maddie into the world that morning. As she emerged, a sudden alarm sounded over the hospital intercom, injecting an unexpected sense of urgency into the room.

Confused and exhausted from the preceding nights, I watched the medical staff rush in with precision. Machines were brought in, suction tubes were placed, and a nurse calmly explained the situation. Something about swallowing meconium—a precautionary measure: initially charged with excitement, the room was now a stage for a different performance.

As the medical staff worked diligently to address the situation, the impending alarm passed, and a sense of calm descended upon the room again—the individuals who had rushed in now exited with measured steps. As the commotion settled, I finally seized the opportunity to embrace those initial, precious moments with my new-born daughter.

Ten days overdue, Madeline Grace German Coulter made her entrance, a tiny 5 lb 14 oz bundle of pure joy. Cradling her in my arms, I looked into her big, beautiful brown eyes. At that moment, a silent exchange unfolded—an unspoken challenge issued by Maddie through an unbroken gaze. It was as if she was saying, *"Daddy, you think this was exciting? We've only just begun."*

Nicole and I had made a pact; she would be called Madeline. It wouldn't be long before she would be affectionately called "Maddie." Honestly, I'd always envisioned her as a Maddie.

That unblinking stare marked the inception of my love for Maddie— a love that would shape our journey through the years and take an unexpected turn.

The enchantment of those first moments with Maddie set the stage for a remarkable journey through parenthood. From the outset, it was evident that Maddie possessed a spirit that would influence everyone around her. The early challenges of her birth were merely a prelude to the resilience and determination she would exhibit throughout her life.

As Maddie grew, so did her unique personality. She was not just a participant in life; she was an active, vibrant force, always setting her course. Every milestone was a testament to her indomitable spirit, from her first steps to her initial words. With Maddie at the centre, Parenthood unfolded like an exhilarating adventure—a journey where love, laughter, and challenges coexisted in perfect harmony.

Our home echoed with Maddie's laughter and the pitter-patter of her tiny feet. Every corner of our lives was touched by her infectious energy, turning ordinary moments into extraordinary memories. As parents, we witnessed our daughter blossom into a unique individual, brimming with dreams and aspirations.

Yet, life, with all its unpredictability, had its plans. Little did we anticipate that this journey, initiated with the radiant glow of Maddie's arrival, would take an unforeseen turn. The idyllic scenes of a happy family would soon confront the harsh reality of teen suicide—a pervasive and devastating issue that lurks in the shadows, affecting families across the globe.

June 28, 2000, the day that marked Maddie's entry into our lives, transformed into a bittersweet milestone. The memories of her birth, once a source of pure joy, now carried a weight of poignant significance. It was a date that split our lives into distinct chapters—the 'before' filled with innocence and hope, and the 'after' marked by the indescribable pain of loss.

The journey took an unexpected detour, and the tranquil scenes of parenthood gave way to the harsh realities of navigating a mental health crisis. Maddie's challenges, though not immediately apparent, silently wove a narrative that would test the strength of our family bonds.

As parents, we were confronted with the stark reality that teen suicide had entered our world, casting a shadow over the once bright pages of our family story. The signs, like subtle whispers, had been there. Maddie's determination, once a source of admiration, now manifested as a relentless internal struggle. The highs and lows of adolescence, magnified by the complexities of mental health, transformed our once-vibrant household into a battlefield of emotions.

As parents, we grappled with the profound helplessness accompanying the realization that our child was facing a formidable adversary.

North York General Hospital marked the starting point, and the finish line symbolized the culmination of a 14-year race, tragically cut short. Our journey, which commenced with the hopeful anticipation of Maddie's birth, concluded with the unbearable weight of a heart-breaking tragedy.

Chapter 2: The Loneliness Epidemic: The Silent Struggle Within Teenage Lives

Our family's story isn't unique. It's essential to grasp what happened to us isn't an isolated incident; the numbers confirm that. While our journey ended tragically, there are countless tales of recovery and triumph. The challenge lies in recognizing the signs. Often, they're subtle, especially in the early stages. Some of you may never face anything similar to our experience, and that's a good thing. The crucial point is that this isn't just about being a parent. Even excellent parenting doesn't guarantee a happy outcome. Conversely, being a less-than-stellar parent doesn't automatically mean your child will face challenges as Maddie did. It might increase the odds, but it's no guarantee.

We can be proactive and raise awareness to get ahead of this issue. Preventative measures can help reduce the risk but don't eliminate it. Our healthcare system is struggling with the burden of our mental health crisis, with resources stretched thin. I aim to impress upon you the seriousness of this crisis. In life, we make choices and take calculated risks; the question here is whether risking the well-being of our loved ones is a gamble worth taking.

WAKE UP YOU COULD LOSE YOUR TEEN TO SUICIDE

Unveiling the Numbers

Picture this: the global landscape reveals a distressing truth—the World Health Organization reports that suicide ranks as the third leading cause of death among individuals aged 15 to 19. Closer to home, in the United States and Canada, the Centers for Disease Control and Prevention deliver a chilling revelation—suicide stands as the second leading cause of death for those between the ages of 10 and 34.

Though cold and impersonal, the numbers mirror a crisis that demands urgent attention. As we delve deeper into the statistics, a concerning pattern emerges—a gendered disparity. While the rate of suicide is higher among males, females are more likely to grapple with suicidal thoughts or attempt to navigate the overwhelming darkness at a rate of almost two to one.

Behind the Masks: Mental Health and Teens

A troubling truth surfaces: a significant portion of teenagers who succumb to suicide carry the weight of mental health disorders. Depression, a silent tormentor, emerges as a prevailing force in these stories. The invisible battles waged within the minds of our youth underscore the need for compassion, understanding, and, above all, effective mental health support systems.

This toll extends to LGBTQ+ youth, who face an elevated risk. The struggle for acceptance and societal challenges creates a crucible of emotional turmoil, adding layers to an already complex issue.

Loneliness: A Silent Epidemic

Let's confront a startling statistic that echoes the silent epidemic within the teenage realm. Several surveys by IMI International dating back to 2015, reveal that a staggering 30% of teens admit to having no real friends. The weight of loneliness, often underestimated, plays a significant role in the mental health landscape of our youth. It amplifies the struggles, making the journey through adolescence a lonely and treacherous path for many.

In a world seemingly more connected than ever, the paradox of isolation looms large. Teens grappling with identity, peer pressure, and societal expectations find solace elusive, leading to a sense of alienation that becomes a breeding ground for despair.

Pete Bombaci and his group, The Genwell Project, are working hard to tackle the problem of loneliness. They want to help Canadians see how being socially isolated, which means being disconnected from or having few ties with others, affects our health.

Understanding this is the first step to making better connections in the future. Loneliness isn't just a feeling—it's also linked to depression, anxiety, and how well we get things done. Pete and his Genwell Project team have made much progress in the last seven years, and the data from the worldwide pandemic supports what they're saying.

Breaking the Silence: A Call to Action

As we navigate these unsettling statistics and narratives, the imperative to break the silence becomes clear. Behind each statistic lies a unique story, a potential turning point that can be shaped by awareness, understanding, and collective action.

Our teens need more than statistical acknowledgment— they need empathetic ears, supportive communities, and mental health resources that bridge the gap between silent suffering and hopeful healing. The rise of teen suicide demands a unified call to action, urging us to be the advocates and allies our youth so desperately need.

In the chapters that follow, we'll explore the underlying factors, the consequences that ripple through communities, and the crucial role of prevention efforts in rewriting the narrative of teen suicide.

It's time to step out of the shadows, confront the harsh realities, and stand together to pursue a safer, more compassionate world for our teens and young adults.

In the Shadows: Cyberbullying and Social Media

Enter the digital world, where teen lives unfold not just in school halls but on screens. Cyberbullying, a silent predator, contributes to the surge in suicidal thoughts and attempts. The constant connectivity of the modern age casts shadows of isolation and torment. Social media, a double-edged sword, offers connection and alienation in equal measure. Excessive use links to heightened feelings of loneliness and depression, creating a virtual world that often deviates from reality. The curated perfection of online lives intensifies the struggles of those battling mental health demons in the shadows.

These statistics will continue to add up, contributing to an aftermath of destruction in its wake. Not only the hordes of lives that will be lost but the devastation of the families and friends reeling as a consequence. We can sit back and let the storm approach, or we can head off the problem before tragedy strikes its unassuming victims, decimating a generation in its path.

Module 2: The Signs

"A parent's love shines brightest when it becomes the beacon of hope in their child's darkest moments."

Chapter 3: Our Actions Have Consequences

Something I now realize is that time and reflection give you perspective. People have often asked me if I would've done anything differently to change the events that transpired on the night of April 10th, 2015. That's a tricky question to try and unravel. Guilt is a natural phenomenon after going through a tragedy like our family has endured.

There isn't a hesitation whether I would've put myself in Maddie's place if given the choice. Survivor's guilt is real, and it is ruthless. I will have to endure it for the rest of my life. Even happy events are shrouded with a heaviness that is unimaginable. I'd be lying if there weren't moments where I've entertained joining Maddie. I'm not ashamed to say that I've concocted plans on how to do it. But the overriding decision is not being able to put my boys through another tragedy, a tragedy that would impact them for the rest of their lives. That would be too selfish to burden them with a legacy of grief. It doesn't mean you don't think about it.

Even though the events that put Maddie's plan in motion go back to December 2014, you can't help but look at what transpired leading up to the catalyst that put things on our radar, at least in reflection.

WAKE UP YOU COULD LOSE YOUR TEEN TO SUICIDE

***

Norine and I steered the ship of Summerlee Office Solutions, a venture I joined back in 1992 as a salesperson. This move came on the heels of the demise of a furniture company I had joined six months earlier. Introduced to Norine Nelson (later Bevan) by a mutual supplier, I instantly connected with her.

Norine and her business partner Jack Summers, the company's founder, ran a small but hearty operation focusing on commodity furniture. Although not initially enthralled by the prospect, I joined the company primarily due to Norine's influence. Eventually, Norine bought out Jack, presenting a new vision for the company—one I could embrace. Over time, my success led to Norine designating me as her heir apparent, offering me a partnership stake in the company.

Aligned and driven, we transformed Summerlee from a $2 million distributor to a formidable $35 million force. Despite starting with a 10% stake, Norine always treated me as a 50/50 partner. Our teamwork drew people in; they believed in our vision and wanted to be part of it. My stake eventually grew to 40%.

Like a big sister, Norine became a source of inspiration and unwavering belief in my capabilities. She was not just a business partner but someone who instilled confidence in my abilities.

As we flourished, a major U.S. supplier courted us, envisioning us as their flagship distributor in Canada.

Recognizing the strategic move, we shifted in 2005, catalyzed by our lead supplier's President undermining my leadership to one of my key employees. This proved hurtful, casting doubts on my capabilities and credibility. It also showed I had much to learn, and that business has no place for fragile egos and hurt feelings. Despite having the most to lose, Norine backed me wholeheartedly.

The transition, supported by a two-year financial safety net from our new supply partner, proved more challenging than anticipated and the next three years tested our resilience until the financial meltdown in 2008, causing us to hemorrhage cash for the first time. We had continually reinvested our profits into the organization, neglecting to substantially pay down personal debt. Depleting our retained earnings, the bank placed us on the credit watch list and called in our line of credit.

Stress levels soared, and for the first time, I battled depression and anxiety. After two years of fighting tooth and nail for survival, Norine and I sat down for lunch, realizing that continuing the business didn't make sense. In February 2010, we made the painful decision to close Summerlee forever. At 44, with three kids aged four to nine, I was unemployed, lost, and walking away with nothing. Yet, the journey, though challenging, held valuable lessons that would shape the chapters yet to unfold.

Within our marriage, imperfections wove themselves into the fabric, and for more than five years, Nicole and I navigated like two ships passing in the night. I bore the weight of my decision— keeping the challenges within our business veiled from Nicole. I justified it as a shield against unnecessary worry, a decision I now recognize as a lapse in judgment. In the midst of a marriage that had lost its vitality, this oversight became a poignant regret, especially considering the four lives intertwined in my decisions.

Confronting our new reality, Nicole and I found ourselves at a crossroads, grappling with the intricate decisions that would shape our family's future. Financially, we stood on precarious ground, having neglected to pay down debt while accumulating more stuff—a standard narrative in Toronto households leveraging home equity to safeguard their children's well-being. With one of our salaries hanging in jeopardy, we realized our financial future was tenuous.

Faced with the urgency of our situation, I sought a consulting gig, contemplating my professional future. Once a focal point, the furniture business now felt lacklustre, prompting a re-evaluation of my options. In the backdrop of financial uncertainties, Nicole and I deliberated the prospect of downsizing our home to alleviate our debt burden. Moving to a smaller residence in our current neighbourhood held little appeal, propelling us to explore the possibility of relocating to the suburbs and joining the ranks of commuters.

Our journey led us to a 5,000 sq. ft haven in Aurora. Nestled beside a golf course, it offered a pool and promised to shed some financial weight. However, it also demanded a move to a new community—this meant a new school, new friends, and a seemingly rejuvenated lease on life, or so I believed. The prospect resonated with the kids, even though it meant disrupting their familiar surroundings. With the sale of our Toronto home, we embarked on a journey north to Aurora, where hopes for a new beginning intertwined with the complexities of change.

Chapter 4: New Location, Same Situation

In the heat of July 2010, our chapter in Aurora began. As the dust settled, our kids seamlessly integrated into their new surroundings. Maddie found her aquatic rhythm with a new swim team, while Zac, wielding his hockey prowess, secured a spot on an Aurora team—a journey I actively participated in as a coaching staff member.

Sawyer embarked on a bilingual pre-kindergarten adventure in his early years, consistent with our commitment to French immersion for Zac and Maddie. Nicole's professional pursuits continued to take her on extensive travels. To mitigate the challenges, we welcomed Eli, a live-in nanny from Brazil, who became a beacon of warmth and unwavering support for our family.

Eli's genuine affection endeared her to all of us, showcasing the profound impact a caregiver can have on a family. Meanwhile, I ventured into uncharted territory, accepting a full-time position with an employee benefit company. This departure from almost two decades of entrepreneurial endeavours presented an opportunity for personal reinvention. The decision, rooted in the necessity to contribute to the family, came with silent reservations. I needed to relaunch and reinvent myself, pulling my financial weight.

Started a new job in a completely new industry. Despite uncertainties, I was thankful for the opportunity and the extra income our family needed.

As summer turned into the school year, our family faced new beginnings. Different schools, sports teams, and the puzzle of change. Surprisingly, we all adjusted quickly and relatively seamlessly.

With our family in three different schools and me commuting to the city daily, life became a complicated dance of balancing work, family, and community. Despite the outward calm, our lives had a different rhythm, defined by the challenges of our daily dance.

The weeks passed, revealing the mix of my feelings—the excitement of hockey culture coexisting with the shadows of depression. While I loved parts of my life, there were clear challenges. Christmas approached, promising a break from the routine, but tensions lingered. Looking back at the pictures, the beautiful home, new friendships, and community couldn't mask the dark depression that weighed on me.

Nicole's career shift to a new firm in the city led to a shared commute to the city—a rare chance to connect in our busy lives. Yet, the silence during those drives spoke volumes about our growing distance. The holiday season, usually joyful, carried an unspoken weight.

On January 3rd, 2011, an ordinary dinner became memorable. Nicole wanted a divorce, addressing what we both felt for a while. The weight of those words hung in the air, but instead of heaviness, I felt relief.

The New Year brought a harsh reality, unravelling the threads that once bound us. As we grappled with this seismic shift, echoes of our past reverberated through our lives. The journey that started with a promise of a new community, schools, and friendships took an unexpected, painful turn, marking the beginning of an even newer chapter about to unfold.

When couples face challenges, some have another child, and others get a dog. We chose to reset in a new community. This would've been okay if we had addressed our relationship challenges. Instead, we painted over the facade with years of little communication. I take responsibility for my part in this failure because no one gets married to get divorced. Still, it's naive to think strong marriages survive without putting in the work to make them thrive. Now, three little souls were exposed in the crossfire.

Chapter 5: The White Elephant Gets Liberated

Surprisingly, after years of near silence, Nicole and I found a way to communicate again. It was as if the very thing that had driven us apart now served as a bridge, allowing us to speak without the weight of awkwardness. The significant barrier that had loomed over our relationship vanished, a silent departure that brought an unexpected sense of relief.

In an effort to shield our kids from the impending storm, we crafted a plan, even though, in retrospect, we understand they may have sensed the changes on the horizon. Our intention was to make the divorce journey as gentle as possible for them, little did we know the emotional tempest awaiting us.

The moment arrived to tell the kids—a task no amount of preparation could fully equip us for. Sitting down with Maddie, almost 11, and Zac, 9, we gently unfolded the news that the strong foundation they'd known since birth was about to shift. Sawyer, at 5, was too young to grasp the magnitude, but his reaction mirrored his older siblings, a collective cry echoing in the room.

Witnessing our children grapple with the forthcoming changes forced us to confront the heart-breaking reality of our decision.

WAKE UP YOU COULD LOSE YOUR TEEN TO SUICIDE

Despite our preparations for the worst, watching our kids navigate through so much pain proved even more challenging than we had anticipated. In just six months, we had turned their lives upside down once, and now we were poised to do it again. The weight of our choices settled on us, underscoring the reasons some parents endure tough times until their kids leave home, attempting to shield them from such significant upheavals.

Children are intuitive, often sensing when something is amiss at home. Even when we believe we're concealing our problems, matters of the heart turn us into poor actors on life's stage. The following five months became a process of unraveling a marriage—a blend of selling possessions, managing kid logistics, and determining how we would navigate life as a separated couple. The journey illuminated both the strength and fragility of family bonds set against the backdrop of emotional turbulence, illustrating how separation can profoundly affect the ones we care about.

For the first time, Maddie began to struggle. The timing was cruel, coinciding with her journey through adolescence, a turbulent period even under the most favourable conditions. Divorce is inherently challenging, and although Nicole and I believed it was the best decision for us, our children would never share our perspective. To them, it was the breaking apart of their world.

Amidst the significant decisions that shape our lives, the choice to return to the city became pivotal, a decision I would later contemplate with quiet regret. At that moment, it felt like a decision for our kids' well-being, a belief that being close to family would aid them in dealing with the changes. As the move approached, we settled in midtown Toronto—a compromise amidst the whirlwind of changes.

The rapid changes marked a period of adaptation and adjustment in our lives. Amidst it all, my daily commute became more manageable, bringing a sense of normalcy. Maddie returned to Toronto French School after a year's hiatus. The boys, now attending a local public school, found comfort in being in the same building. The older two handled the changes relatively well, but Sawyer struggled with his emotions. Separation and anxiety, exacerbated by our divorce, made it tough for him. Grades one and four at John Fisher became the new chapter for Sawyer and Zac, while Maddie continued grade six at TFS.

Maddie, a source of joy and well-liked, easily rekindled friendships with her unique and bold sense of humour and likability. Unlike the usual dynamics among young girls, she steered clear of gossip and cliques, maintaining a refreshing honesty and straightforwardness. Maddie treated everyone equally, unbothered by popularity contests. She stood out as a leader; a role that would only become clear later.

Without being entangled in the drama often associated with private schools, Maddie's confidence was impressive for her age. She didn't seek to impress; instead, she led by example. Her aversion to judgment became a defining trait. Maddie's leadership was quiet but powerful, countering the drama of teenage interactions. Little did we realize back then that her skill in navigating social situations would leave a lasting impact on those around her—a legacy of authenticity and inclusivity.

However, changing schools, shuttling between two different homes every week, and coming to terms with the sudden realization that her parents were now living under separate roofs proved to be a challenging journey for our once-upbeat, happy-go-lucky girl. The turmoil had begun.

Chapter 6: There's No Such Thing as a Good Time for Divorce

Nobody walks down the aisle, exchanging vows, thinking of an exit strategy. The casualties of divorce are extensive—children, assets, and the emotional baggage carried along. Suddenly, expenses double while you're left with a single disposable income. Divorce has a way of bringing out the worst in people. Children and money can turn even the most pragmatic individuals into two UFC fighters squaring off in the ring. It's perplexing how someone once revered as a life partner can turn nasty. We've all heard the horror stories of divorce, and unfortunately, the kids often become casualties of this war. The very thing that once united a marriage—love—becomes a catalyst for tearing it apart.

Navigating Divorce with Empathy: Raw Emotion and Its Impact on Kids

Raw and heated emotion can drive a wedge of irreparable damage into a once-beautiful relationship. To say that your kids won't be impacted is naive, even if you shield them from the bitterness. Nurturing your children through divorce is about understanding the impact and prioritizing their well-being.

Divorce is a challenging experience that affects not only the couple involved but also their children. Recognizing the emotional toll it takes on kids and prioritizing their well-being is crucial. We want to eliminate the impact of divorce on children and figure out a way to minimize its harmful effects and promote their healthy development. We also highlight the importance of cohesive parental support, even in adversity.

Fostering a Positive Co-Parenting Dynamic:

During and after divorce, maintaining a respectful and amicable relationship with your ex-spouse is essential, especially in the presence of your children. While it may be difficult, avoiding constant nit-picking, competition, and criticism is vital. Shielding your kids from unnecessary conflict will significantly reduce their emotional burden and provide a more stable environment.

Minimizing Emotional Exposure and Blame:

Children should never feel responsible for their parent's divorce.

Separating your grievances from your role as a parent is crucial. Put your ego aside and focus on creating a nurturing atmosphere where your child feels loved and supported. Avoid turning your child into a pawn or using them as a means to win against your ex-spouse. Remember, their well-being should always be the priority.

This is all fine and good, but we are not machines. We are subject to emotional volatility. We are not immune to occasional emotional outbursts, feelings of contempt toward our former spouse and acts that we may not be proud of doing.

Cohesion and Love Amidst Challenges:

While divorce introduces significant changes, it is possible to demonstrate cohesive parental support for the sake of your child's well-being. Early on in the process, we did a commendable job. Setting aside bitterness and hatred can create a united front when dealing with challenging situations. Sharing the responsibility of supporting your children through difficult times, such as illness or mental health struggles, can provide them with a sense of stability and reassurance.

Putting Your Child's Needs First:

Above all, remember that your child deserves to feel both parents' love focused on them. By prioritizing your child's well-being, you can create an environment where they feel secure and loved, regardless of the challenges surrounding your divorce. Show them that their happiness and emotional health remain at the forefront despite differences. Remember that your children didn't decide to get divorced; we chose that path.

Chapter 7: Navigating the Emotional Roller Coaster: The Unseen Impact on Parents

The emotional roller coaster of divorce doesn't just affect children; it takes a toll on parents, too. The vision of a lifelong partnership shatters, leaving individuals to pick up the pieces while trying to guide their children through the chaos. The journey through divorce is not a linear path; it's a series of highs and lows, each presenting its unique challenges. There isn't a handbook on navigating the perils of divorce for parents.

Understanding the Emotional Toll on Parents: Coping with Loss

Divorce marks the end of a significant chapter in one's life, bringing a sense of loss, failure, and grief. The dream of a shared future dissipates, replaced by the daunting task of creating a new normal. The emotional toll on parents can manifest as sadness, anger, guilt, and anxiety. Navigating these emotions while supporting children requires a delicate balance.

Personally, the preeminent emotions for me were shame and guilt.

It is something that continues to plague me on some level, even though I've gone through extensive counselling to address it. There is no such thing as a *"one-and-done"* therapy session. Admittedly, men are not as accepting or welcoming as women to therapy. Many guys, if they attend counselling, don't realize more work goes into these sessions post-appointment. There's no magic formula, and you don't get better by only showing up. Most guys don't like a mirror put a foot away from their face and told to look closely at it when taking responsibility for the fallout of a marriage.

Vulnerability, honesty, and acceptance take time, yet very few men admit needing help. Divorce was another added to my list of failures accompanying my failed business. With each failure, it chipped away at my already fragile confidence. This is what depression does to your psyche.

Seeking Professional Support: Therapeutic Guidance for Emotional Healing

Acknowledging the emotional weight of divorce is the first step. Seeking professional support, such as therapy or counselling, provides a structured space to navigate complex emotions. Therapists can offer coping strategies, communication tools, and a non-judgmental environment for parents to process their feelings.

Truthfully, I struggled. I hadn't completely dealt with the loss of my business. To a large extent, this meant having my identity stripped of me. Some of it was ego, but a more significant part was shame. When you have something that you've poured your heart and soul into for twenty years and suddenly ripped it out of your life, it becomes like this phantom limb that has been amputated from your body. The daily routine and predictable income stream get disrupted. You are forced to go into survival mode. This was my baby before I had kids. Even though it represented a different kind of love, there was an internal pride in saying I ran my own business. I felt less worthy. I was always a pretty confident person, but now I felt fragile.

Shame represents a delicate balance between feeling like you've let your family and yourself down. The other part of the emotional equation is this feeling of guilt. I tried to overcompensate for feeling this shame by being the best dad I could be for the kids. This meant overcommitting to my involvement with them. That decision will never be part of my regret.

Building Emotional Resilience and Dating Again

Divorce brings an onslaught of challenges, but developing healthy coping mechanisms is crucial for emotional resilience. Engaging in activities that bring joy, maintaining social connections, and prioritizing self-care contribute to one's emotional well-being. As parents build emotional resilience, they become better equipped to support their children through the transition.

Likely, this impacted my emotional resilience when putting myself out there and dating again. The adage that you can't love another person until you learn to love yourself is so applicable.

Even though you think you are ready to move on and find love, the heart must heal before it can move on healthily.

Looking back now, you can't replace an emotional void until all the scars of your last relationship are healed. If you don't address this first, you will just leave a trail of carnage in your wake.

Effective Co-Parenting: Navigating Challenges with Empathy

Co-parenting after divorce requires a commitment to effective communication and empathy. Understanding that both parents play vital roles in a child's life fosters a sense of stability. Open communication about parenting decisions, consistency in routines, and a united front during challenging times contribute to a healthier co-parenting dynamic.

We had a schedule of one week on and one week off. Later, it would be moved to a two-week on and two-week off schedule. Those significant gaps between living with parents can feel like an eternity for young kids. Also, as we experienced with Sawyer, transitioning between households can be difficult. Nicole's travel schedule precluded a two-week schedule, which was logistically the only option. Kids not having access to both parents can prove challenging. Kids learn to manipulate circumstances to suit their own needs. For me, as Maddie was going through adolescence, she tended to *"milk"* the menstruation cramps issue often. It was unrelatable for me, and Maddie tended to play me. There were a lot of Google Searches and leaning on Caroline and her girls to help navigate the pubescent girl labyrinth.

Creating a New Narrative: Shaping a Positive Post-Divorce Future

Moving beyond the emotional turmoil of divorce involves creating a new narrative for oneself and the family. Focusing on personal growth, setting new goals, and embracing change can pave the way for a positive post-divorce future. Sharing these aspirations with children helps them see that life continues, filled with possibilities.

The emotional landscape of divorce is intricate, impacting both parents and children. Parents can empathize with the complexities by understanding and addressing the emotional toll. Seeking professional support, developing healthy coping mechanisms, prioritizing effective co-parenting, and shaping a positive post-divorce narrative contribute to emotional healing and resilience. While divorce is undoubtedly challenging, it also presents an opportunity for personal growth and the construction of a new, fulfilling chapter in life.

Chapter 8: Balancing Act: Navigating Finances and Fostering Joyful Activities

Divorce is more than an emotional roller coaster; it's a financial juggernaut, and entrepreneurs navigating this terrain face a particularly daunting challenge. Imagine being an entrepreneur dealing with insolvency, trying to rebuild not just your career but your entire life. Some days felt like staring down a firing squad every morning, and just getting out of bed was an accomplishment in itself.

Finding Balance: Nurturing Purpose and Joy in Kids' Activities

In our bustling world, keeping our kids engaged in activities that bring purpose and physical vitality is crucial. It's not just about sports; any focused activity, like playing a musical instrument, can profoundly benefit their mental health.

Consider Maddie, a competitive swimmer training six days a week at the provincial level. When she wanted to quit, we, as parents, gave in too quickly. Perhaps returning to her training level while emphasizing the joy of the sport might have been wiser. After all, exercise, in any form, acts as an exceptional antidepressant for everyone.

However, we must be wary of the slippery slope that losing purpose and focus creates. High-level activities can burden young individuals with immense pressure, stripping away their joy. Balancing our children's aspirations with their overall well-being is vital.

Striking this balance ensures they continue finding fulfilment in their chosen activities. It's not about pushing them beyond their limits; it's about creating an environment where they thrive, enjoy the process, and grow physically and mentally.

The Impact on Maddie's Swimming Journey

All our kids were athletic. The boys excelled in hockey, soccer, and baseball, while Maddie was a standout swimmer. She dominated in the pool, winning multiple gold medals in meets. Her dedication was immense, training six days a week at the Provincial level. She swam like a dolphin in early mornings, 90-minute sessions, boosting her confidence.

We attended all her meets, cheering her on as she anchored relay teams and led her peers. The pool, surrounded by friends, had been her happy place for years. But one day, everything changed. During a two-day meet, Maddie, typically effortless in the water, suddenly needed more will to compete. It was as if someone turned off her competitive spirit.

After not making the podium on the first day, she pleaded not to go back for the second. I relented too quickly. Sadly, that marked the end of her swimming journey. Looking back, we could've taken a swimming *"timeout"* with Maddie, revisiting the commitment later. If the feelings persisted after a short break, we could've reset expectations or dropped to a less competitive loop requiring less commitment. Like work, where we don't quit because of a challenging day or two, revisiting expectations could have been an option. There are many decisions I've questioned, but for that particular one, I'd like to request a do-over.

In this journey, we realized that engaging our kids in purposeful activities is more than medals or podiums; it's about nurturing their passion and joy. It's about allowing them to find their rhythm, encouraging them to pursue their interests, and helping them understand that the essence of any activity lies in the joy it brings. As parents, it's our responsibility to guide them through this delicate balance, ensuring their chosen activities contribute positively to their growth and well-being. After all, the true victory lies in winning competitions, self-discovery, and personal development.

Chapter 9: When School Becomes a Burden

Maddie had consistently excelled both academically and athletically, her popularity spanning various circles—school, swimming, camp, and the cottage. With an unconventional spirit and a strong moral compass, she was a teenager with a will that occasionally clashed with her parents.

As our separation unfolded, the dynamics between Nicole and me became strained, a shift keenly sensed by the kids despite our efforts to shield them. Maddie, who had never resisted attending school, began showing signs of reluctance. The morning routine became a struggle, and her academic performance suffered. While the early stages of our separation seemed relatively smooth, the cracks were now visible.

Challenges extended beyond her academic life. Maddie's resistance to getting out of bed and participating in family activities intensified. She retreated to her room, spending more time on her phone—her newfound confidant—conversing with friends over FaceTime. Despite my encouragement for her to join family walks and activities, she chose solitude. It was evident that something was amiss.

During this period, I respected Maddie's need for space, hesitant to disrupt the delicate balance. It became clear that I was punching above my weight class. The infectious laughter and spirited sense of humour that defined our happy-go-lucky teenager became less prominent. Her smile, once a constant presence, faded. The vibrant spirit we all cherished seemed to be dimming. The question loomed: what had happened to our once carefree young girl?

The Tragic New School Year

Maddie's educational journey began at Toronto French School, a financial gift from Nicole's parents that provided her with a strong foundation. Her early exposure to Montessori education in our old neighbourhood had set her on a path where reading and math came naturally. With her academically advanced going into Grade One, we felt she would grow bored and stagnate. The prospect of learning in an all-French environment was a good compromise. Adorned in her little grey tunic and braided hair, she entered Grade One at TFS with her angelic traits.

French immersion suited her well; she enthusiastically shared her newfound vocabulary every afternoon. Maddie thrived at TFS, embracing the learning environment until the end of Grade Eight. However, circumstances abruptly shifted; the private school funding was cut off, and for the first time since Kindergarten, Maddie was enrolled in a public school— North Toronto Collegiate Institute.

This transition marked a significant change and seemed to contribute to her growing sadness, manifesting in prolonged bouts of acting out and behavioural challenges. Parties became a way for Maddie to navigate her new social landscape, exposing her to alcohol and intensifying her defiance. I vividly recall picking her up from a house party, where parents had hired security to manage the crowd outside, resembling more of a Western Homecoming party than an innocent Grade Eight gathering.

The party scene became a weekly affair, introducing strict curfews and tense conversations into our lives. Weekends, once a time of relaxation, transformed into periods of heightened anxiety. I eagerly anticipated the weeks Maddie stayed with her mom, as it offered a temporary respite from the unexplainable challenges that seemed to escalate each weekend. My anxiety soared, and the once-anticipated weekends now filled me with a sense of dread.

CHRIS COULTER

Chapter 10: The First Attempt or a Cry for Help?

Navigating adolescence is like riding a rollercoaster—full of unexpected twists, challenges, and moments of deep concern. Maddie, typically a dedicated student in ninth grade, found herself in a different academic story. Her once high grades plummeted as indifference towards school took hold, revealing an unsettling inner struggle that two years of counselling couldn't completely unravel.

Thinking about Maddie's journey took me back to my teenage years and the challenges my parents likely faced during my escapades. One fall day, with exam pressure looming, I invited Maddie to join us at Zac's hockey game. Instead, she chose to stay home, citing the need to study.

Returning home after the game, Maddie's absence set off alarms. Unreachable by phone, rumours hinted at a gathering in Hoggs Hollow, raising suspicions she might be there. In a chaotic house pulsating with energy and flowing alcohol, I found myself pushing through the party, reminiscent of a scene from Uncle Buck, navigating the pandemonium to locate my daughter.

WAKE UP YOU COULD LOSE YOUR TEEN TO SUICIDE

Finally finding Maddie, her demeanour revealed the influence of substances, making the task of coaxing her away delicate. *"Are you mad at me?"* she constantly asked.

"Let's talk about it tomorrow. Let's get you home and to bed," I replied. The fine line between parent and confidant was being tested, and concerns echoed through my thoughts.

Tucking Maddie into bed as the boys slept peacefully, I reassured her that a new and better day awaited. Exhausted from the night's events and the elusive nature of sleep in the post-separation landscape. Approaching Maddie's room at 9 am, I found the door firmly locked. Opting to give her more time to sleep off the effects of the night before, I focused on the boys' breakfast.

A peculiar sight disrupted the routine—a spill of pills scattered on the kitchen floor. A disquieting realization hit me—had Maddie taken these pills? Concern heightened as I returned to her door, knocking violently without a response. Putting my shoulder into the door, the prospect of unthinkable scenarios loomed large as it gave way.

Inside, Maddie lay unconscious, surrounded by a chaotic collection of pills and a bottle of vodka. Rushing to her, I tried to wake her, checking for signs of life. Groggy but breathing, she remained with us. A frantic call to 911 initiated the agonizing wait for the ambulance, each passing moment laden with a mixture of fear and relief.

Being a parent felt fragile, stretched by unexpected challenges and powerful moments that mixed up the roles of taking care and protecting. As Maddie went through her experiences, it showed how strong you have to be when being a parent goes beyond the usual. By understanding and sharing feelings, the story became a mix of being open about the struggles of a parent who worries and a teenager searching for who they are and where they fit in.

The hum of daily life in our quiet Don Mills neighbourhood was shattered that fateful day. It started with the arrival of paramedics; their white and blue vehicles starkly contrasted against the serene backdrop. Following closely were the fire truck and the police, their presence drawing a curious crowd of neighbours—some genuinely concerned, others merely driven by curiosity.

We had settled into this peaceful neighbourhood in the summer of 2012, our haven in the form of a quiet cul-de-sac. While I knew my immediate neighbours by name, the relationships were more cordial than close-knit. Ours was a family that largely kept to itself, the boys honing their hockey skills on the driveway and my car becoming a familiar sight, shuttling the kids to various activities.

As the paramedics ushered Maddie into the ambulance, the absence of blaring sirens offered a fragile reassurance. Irony lingered in the air—a silent ambulance carrying my daughter to North York General Hospital, a mere five-minute drive away, a place that had once resonated with joy as the birthplace of all three of my children.

The busy emergency room welcomed Maddie's stretcher, but underneath the hurried atmosphere was a mix of personal struggles. It was around 10:30 am, and things were less chaotic than usual. Maddie got a quick check to ensure her vital signs were okay, and the emergency doctor said she wasn't in immediate danger.

Then came the questions, digging into a painful truth. My 14-year-old daughter, overwhelmed by despair, had tried to take her own life. The weight of this revelation hung in the air, showing that a harsh reality existed beneath our seemingly ordinary lives. The emergency doctor explained the standard procedure—Maddie needed an assessment by the resident psychiatrist.

In the middle of all this, I realized I hadn't told Nicole, who was in New York. A quick call reassured her that Maddie's life wasn't at immediate risk, and she hurriedly booked a flight home.

The psychiatrist talked to Maddie, her alertness sharply contrasting with the turmoil inside. They had a detailed conversation, showing how serious the situation was. The doctor decided it was necessary to admit her under Form One, a request for a psychiatric assessment. This step was crucial to figure out if Maddie needed more care in a psychiatric facility. In simpler terms, Maddie's journey was far from over.

One haunting question sealed her admission: *"When you realized you weren't successful in your attempt on your life, were you relieved or disappointed?"* Maddie's response echoed disappointment, casting a sombre shadow over the unfolding narrative.

The Youth Adolescent Mental Health Unit on the seventh floor became an unexpected chapter in our lives—a place we would become intimately acquainted with over the next five months. Little did we know that this space, teeming with stories of resilience and recovery, would become the backdrop of Maddie's journey toward healing.

Chapter 11 Our Home on 7 North

The Youth Adolescent Psychiatric Unit, fondly known as 7 North, unexpectedly transformed into a haven for our family. Three years had passed since our departure from Aurora, and in this clinical and sterile space, Nicole and I set aside our differences. Our shared mission was simple: to ensure our daughter left this place healthier and, hopefully, happier.

While the physical surroundings of 7 North were sterile, the warmth and support emanating from the people within were palpable. This temporary community, grappling with various challenges, guarded the privacy of their stories. The reasons for each admission remained a mystery unless someone chose to share. Despite diverse struggles, a common thread emerged—everyone sought support and found solace within these walls, promising safety.

Units like 7 North were designed for acute situations, offering a brief respite for those facing immediate threats. Stays were short, emphasizing the temporary nature of these spaces. Long-term assistance fell upon external entities, often private agencies or not-for-profits. Unfortunately, the demand for such services surpassed the available supply, exposing systemic challenges in mental health support.

Maddie didn't merely adapt to 7 North; she swept through like a force of nature. Her infectious enthusiasm endeared her to staff and fellow patients alike. Maddie possessed a natural inclusivity, committing to positively impact any space she inhabited, despite her internal struggles. The sterile walls bore witness to the arrival of a new resident, and Maddie's presence resonated in the most uplifting way imaginable. In no time, she became the darling of the unit.

It was as if Maddie held an invisible clipboard dedicated to catalyzing positive change. Her boundless enthusiasm injected fresh air into the unit, fostering an environment where everyone felt valued. Maddie, the unofficial greeter, would declare, *"I'm Maddie,"* accompanied by a radiant smile. Her presence became a beacon of reassurance for patients and parents who, burdened with fear, entered the unit. Maddie's charm had an uncanny ability to dispel the anxieties that often accompanied such challenging circumstances.

Not every moment on 7 North was cheerful. Maddie still grappled with moments of sadness and depression, often concealed from her fellow patients. In the privacy of her room, the vibrant Maddie would sometimes retreat into darkness and introspection. Remembering why she was there is essential—to heal and leave that underlying sadness behind.

Despite the challenges, Maddie encountered dedicated and exceptional practitioners at 7 north. One individual who played a pivotal role as a youth counsellor was Kadeem. When Maddie found herself in the depths of her dark abyss, it was Kadeem who could help her climb out. Their bond was unique, marked by exchanges filled with laughter and genuine connection. Kadeem's qualities, marked by relatability and empathy, had a calming effect that made you instantly feel secure—a feeling Maddie desperately needed.

While Nicole, the boys, and I couldn't be at 7 North every hour, knowing Kadeem was there provided solace. Among the many remarkable individuals on the unit, Kadeem stood out for the hope he instilled in Maddie. Ten days after her arrival, Maddie received the all-clear to go home—a pre-Christmas gift that brought joy and relief to our family. Santa came a week early this year.

The Whole Family Home for Christmas

Maddie left the hospital to stay at my place with the boys. There was a palpable nervousness in the air, a collective awareness that we were re-entering familiar but recently fraught territory. The past two weeks' events had made us realize life's fragility, and I found myself tiptoeing around Maddie, cautious not to trigger any distress. Returning to the space where Maddie must have felt desperately alone was daunting.

To create a safer environment, I *"Maddie-proofed"* my home. The alcohol and prescription drugs were purged, her bedroom door repaired, and her room meticulously cleaned. Yet, the reality lingered – if someone wanted to find a way to harm themselves, they likely would. Balancing this concern, we aimed not to coddle Maddie excessively. Maintaining the genuine edginess, humour, and banter that defined our family dynamic was crucial.

Upon her return, Maddie presented a calmer, softer, and more subdued version of her usual self. Whether influenced by the prescribed drugs or the weight of the recent experiences sinking in, the transformation was evident. The boys, thrilled to have her home, eagerly embraced her presence. Maddie was their ringleader, bringing life and laughter to our home. The familiar sibling banter between Sawyer and Maddie resumed while Zac, her loyal confidante, remained by her side, engaging in quiet conversations. Gradually, life began to regain a sense of normalcy, although my anxiety lingered.

As a family, we ventured out to get a Christmas tree, spending an evening decorating it together. This simple act, a cherished tradition, marked a step toward reclaiming our *"new normal."* Per Maddie's wishes, the incident had been kept under wraps outside our immediate family. To the outside world, Maddie had been hospitalized for some undisclosed stomach issues – a more straightforward narrative than the complex reality we faced. While it felt uncomfortable, we respected Maddie's need for privacy.

Communicating with Maddie's school about her missed exams, we found them supportive, granting her an indefinite reprieve. This compassionate response eased some of the academic pressures. The school suggested an adjusted and reduced schedule, emphasizing a gradual return in the New

WAKE UP YOU COULD LOSE YOUR TEEN TO SUICIDE

Year or whenever Maddie felt ready. The collective efforts to preserve Maddie's well-being became a shared commitment as we navigated the path toward healing and recovery together.

Christmas and New Year's unfolded in the familiar pattern of alternating celebrations between Nicole and me. The kids gracefully shuffled between our homes, creating a unique holiday season. Unlike the typical two-week schedule, this year saw a more frequent exchange of kids between our households. After the New Year, we anticipated returning to our usual routine, a semblance of normalcy.

The kids gradually settled back into their regular routines as the weeks passed. School resumed its regular cadence, though Maddie needed more time to be ready to dive back into the academic environment. Conversely, the boys eagerly embraced the second half of their school year – Sawyer continued Grade 4 and Zac resumed Grade 7.

During this period, the kids spent a couple of weeks with Nicole. Left alone with my thoughts, I grappled with the illusion that life was returning to normal. An underlying uneasiness persisted, and my struggles with sleeplessness continued. Turning to Gravol for aid, I found it helped me fall asleep but failed to maintain a restful slumber.

The two weeks passed swiftly, and soon; the kids were back under my roof in the early days of January. Nicole resumed her travel routine, heading back to New York. The ebb and flow of our lives resumed, yet the lingering unease hinted at the complexities looming beneath the surface.

We kept trying to involve Maddie, but she seemed unsure. The boys treated her kindly, but I was careful not to upset her. When words failed, I gave her hugs in her room. She said she was okay, but as a parent, I worried and found it hard to relax and sleep. Maddie's usual joy had faded, and our attempts to make her happy felt delicate.

Sometimes, we forget about threats with time. Maddie and I liked watching old movies like *"Stand by Me," "Fletch," "Stripes," "Uncle Buck,"* and *"Princess Bride."* Maddie loved these movie nights, and I treasure those memories. It was our special time while the boys were busy doing their own thing.

Even with everything going on, Maddie and I continued our movie nights. We liked classics that gave us a break from reality. *"Stand By Me"* meant more to us, *"Fletch"* made us laugh, and *"Stripes"* taught us about sticking together. *"Uncle Buck"* and *"Princess Bride"* showed us the power of love. Our movie nights weren't just for fun; they were a safe place where we put aside worries, at least for a couple of hours.

In those tough times, *saying "I love you"* became important. Maddie held onto that love, and our movie nights became a lifeline, a place where we forgot the world outside and the stresses associated with it.

WAKE UP YOU COULD LOSE YOUR TEEN TO SUICIDE

But deep down, we knew things were different. Life was fragile, and even simple moments felt heavy. Our usual routine seemed out of reach.

As we faced challenges, our family stayed strong with love and courage. Every day, we balance the present and the unknown. Even though the laughter wasn't as prevalent as it once was, love held us together. In that love, we found the strength to face tough times and be there for each other.

The night before the second attempt is a blur in my memory. We went to bed like any other evening, and I can't recall if we had hockey or if Maddie and I watched a movie together. There were no triggering events—no alcohol, no turbulent incidents, no expressions of anger or overwhelming sadness. It was the carefree evening that preceded it that raised my biggest concern. I went to bed with my guard down, waking up unsuspecting.

In the morning, I woke up the boys and then Maddie. Something felt off as I entered Maddie's room. I didn't realize anything was amiss until I opened the curtains to let in some sunlight. Maddie's bottle of antidepressants and a bottle of gin were in the room, even though I had removed most of the pills and alcohol from the house. I'm unsure of what prompted another attempt on Maddie's part, and that uncertainty adds to the distress in hindsight.

I don't comprehend where the mind goes when deciding to end one's life, especially when it seems so random and unnecessary. Despite lacking the means to achieve her goal, the attempt was genuine. She was conscious and alert, though disappointed when I woke her up—not disappointed that I disturbed her sleep but disappointed that she could be awakened.

This time, there was no need to summon emergency services. We got into my car and drove to the hospital ourselves: no sirens, no neighbours, no garnering of attention. We entered the Emergency Department of North York General Hospital, familiar with the process, knowing that 7 North would soon be our home for the foreseeable future.

Chapter 13: The Return to 7 North

When patients leave 7 North, the staff probably wish they never have to see them there again. Maddie, a force of nature, brought vibrance to the unit, but they didn't want her to return, as readmission meant she had tried to harm herself again. Severe depression is complex, with many layers and unpredictability. You might go to bed feeling great and wake up with the world's weight on your chest. It's unexplainable and unyielding. Living with depression can make you feel unmotivated, uninspired, and ungrateful. Finding the good in any situation becomes hard, no matter how much you try.

The second admission to 7 North was more brutal than before. Our happy little greeter from before Christmas wasn't the same. There was an overriding sadness this time. Maddie wasn't as engaged; her bright eyes were darker with indifference. She didn't want to be here, but sadly, she didn't want to be anywhere. She responded to her friend Kadeem and her brothers but was pretty unresponsive to everyone else.

Upon Maddie's being readmitted, I immediately notified Nicole. She came home, sensing this setback was different than before. This time, it wasn't a cry for help.

Maddie shared her deepest, darkest emotions, desiring not to live another day. I remember being unable to control my emotions, pleading with her to want to live while sobbing uncontrollably. As a parent, seeing your child suffer is painful, but Maddie's primary objective was the opposite to what we wanted. It was like the light had dimmed on her desire to live. Nicole and I knew this stay would be an extended version of the previous one. This was going to test all our resolve.

Nicole, the boys, and I visited Maddie every day. The boys never complained, knowing their presence lifted Maddie's spirits. They brought much-needed laughter and fun to 7 north. I tried to be positive, happy, and resourceful, but watching this beautiful 14year-old struggle to see the next sunrise was devastating.

Respecting Maddie's wish to keep her hospital stay reason secret, we stuck to the story about prolonged stomach issues. We faced many concerns about her wellbeing from her friends. The most significant gap was not having access to her phone. In reflection, letting some of her close friends understand her situation might have given her more hope and optimism.

Today, knowing that 60% of young women go through extended episodes of anxiety and depression might have created a more understanding environment among her friends, sparking honest conversations and a sense of togetherness. Misery doesn't necessarily love company but finding solace in not going through things alone can make a difference. Having personally dealt with these feelings for the last 15 years, there's a feeling of shame, guilt, and loneliness that's hard to talk about sometimes.

WAKE UP YOU COULD LOSE YOUR TEEN TO SUICIDE

The daily visits helped Maddie. We started seeing glimpses of Maddie's old spirit. Laughter and humour started reappearing. Maddie regained her role as the unofficial greeter on the unit, welcoming new patients and parents unfamiliar with 7 North. She became an unofficial therapist, helping establish trust with other patients and breaking down barriers. This gave her purpose and meaning, finding fulfilment in helping others. She also wanted changes in the sterile environment of 7 North, like greater access to the outdoors and fresh air. She felt exercise or wellness equipment would promote a more positive and faster recovery. The confines of 7 North were apparent, restricting her world to the 4,000 square feet of the unit. By this point, Maddie had been there for over a month for her second stay.

Discussions started about opening up her world to the outside, starting with short visits to Starbucks in the hospital foyer. Beyond this, there were talks about accompanying access to outdoor walks and visits to Nicole and my homes. It was progress, something we all longed for in the future.

The prospect of a temporary break from the confines of 7 north boosted Maddie's spirits. Our daily trip to Starbucks became something we both looked forward to. It may have been a small step, but considering where we were just a month earlier, it was a cause for celebration. This temporary freedom allowed Maddie to savour her caffeinated and chocolate-filled treat outside the unit, allowing us to enter the brisk February weather, even for an hour. It lifted both our spirits and the promise of more extended leaves.

The staff still discouraged Maddie from bringing her phone on our Starbucks outings, and truthfully, I cherished the uninterrupted time together. We were witnessing the revival of our girl's spirits, and for the first time in over a month, I started to see the potential for a positive outcome. I wasn't naive enough to think we were entirely out of the woods, but I considered it progress, even if we were only inching forward daily. Forward was undoubtedly better than backward.

Maddie's conversations began to involve a future state, a significant shift from the present-day focus of previous talks. It didn't mean the tough days were entirely behind us, but there were noticeably fewer challenging days every week. The challenge with being at 7 North or any psychiatric unit is that they are designed for emergencies or acute situations, needing more capacity or resources for long-term care. The expectation was to transition to an intermediary agency for management beyond immediate danger. However, these agencies were limited and beyond capacity, making navigating the mental health care system virtually impossible. Mental health resources haven't kept pace with demand, becoming an increasing problem for our fragile healthcare system.

We were assigned to Youth dale, a mental health care agency for youth, young adults, and families with complex needs. The challenge was that they assessed candidates on a triage basis and then determined bed availability. Weekly calls from the onboarding team asked about Maddie's well-being, and my responses depended on the emotional rollercoaster of her week. Meanwhile, Maddie stayed on 7 north, even though the typical stay varied from a few days to a few weeks. After being there for over a month, we explored options to transition her to another facility.

Many mental health facilities catering to Maddie's needs were more focused on drug and alcohol addiction than severe depressive episodes. Navigating this system was painful, frustrating, and maddening. There's nothing worse than feeling like you're on a hamster wheel every day, searching for something that will help save your child's life.

Every day brought renewed hope and promise, with little victories moving us forward in a positive direction and opening up increased opportunities and privileges. They started issuing four-hour passes, allowing us to leave the hospital property.

I remember a day when Maddie was out on a pass from the hospital. She loved her lattes from the in-hospital Starbucks, but she especially looked forward to her day passes to go home. One afternoon, on a pass, she was at my house, just the two of us. The conversation was light, and she was kicking my butt in Anomia, a game she played with vigour and enthusiasm. It was a game she seldom lost at playing, and that day was no exception; she proceeded to annihilate me in quick fashion. Then something happened, like a storm coming in off the ocean, darkness came over her. She said, *"Daddy, you must take me back to the hospital."* I didn't know what suddenly overcame her, but she realized she was in danger. At that moment, she felt a threat from within herself.

I don't pretend to understand how she felt that day or on several occasions leading up to that fateful evening on April 10th, but the pain she felt was real. Maddie was trying to protect the ones she loved the most at the sacrifice of herself. This sudden transformation scared her, and it scared me. We had seen so much progress since the time she had been admitted, but something happened that day that was indescribable. It was our progress's first test in a couple of weeks. All those milestones in moving forward had now been brought into question. Every ounce of my fibre wanted to believe she was getting better, but that day cast a severe shadow of a doubt that we were almost beyond this looming threat.

We worked towards more frequent day passes in the following weeks, aiming for eventual overnights away from 7 North. Our stay at the hospital had become quite extended by this point. During this time, we met with practitioners, and there was optimism about transitioning Maddie into a day patient. This meant being at the hospital during the day and staying at either Nicole's or my place at night. The hope was to eliminate the hospital from our day-to-day routine eventually. They would work on various coping strategies during the hospital days to ensure a permanent departure for Maddie. Although there was still a long way to go, at least there was an endgame to work towards.

WAKE UP YOU COULD LOSE YOUR TEEN TO SUICIDE

A call from Youth dale informed us that a bed had opened up. Youth dale residents typically stayed voluntarily for a month to a year. Nicole, Maddie, and I decided to check out the facility downtown. After a tour and an explanation of the program, we learned about a typical stay for a resident youth. After seeing the facilities, we mutually agreed that this might be a step back for Maddie. We decided to pass on the opportunity and declined the offered bed. Around the same time, Maddie became a day patient at 7 north. We would drop her off by 9 am, pick her up by 4 pm, and bring her home.

Until this point, she had spent ten days on 7 North before Christmas and two months from the end of January until the end of March, at which point she would transition to being a day patient.

It's often been said that if you have two choices, you have an option; if you have one thing to choose from, you have a dilemma. By abandoning the Youth dale option, we were banking on the 7 North Out-patient option as the right choice. We continued to explore other treatment options, but none presented themselves. We'll never know if we chose correctly but choosing Youth dale seemed like the wrong option for Maddie. Had a bed been available earlier on our journey, would we have had a different opinion? I've tried not to get anguished over those hypothetical situations, mainly because they weren't available when we needed them most. In my heart, we were grateful for the support we received on 7 north. Everyone in that unit did everything they could to help our daughter and family.

The events leading up to the fateful evening on April 10th have been discussed and deliberated at length. Sometimes, love for a child is not enough; ultimately, the child has the choice of how to live or not live their life. No single person bears the finger of blame. Multiple factors have contributed to Maddie making her ultimate decision.

The real purpose of this story is not to overthink what happened to our daughter because that story will not change, but instead to share the valuable lessons in parenting so that, hopefully, another family doesn't have to endure the same pain that we will always endure.

Module 3: The Lessons

"The importance of lessons from parenting lies not only in what we teach our children but in what they teach us about ourselves."

Chapter 13: A Father's Path to Understanding, Sharing, and Healing

We chose to keep our ordeal with Maddie private, honouring her wishes as we navigated our hell in solitude. Only a select few were privy to the depths of what we were going through with Maddie. While their intentions to help were sincere, we found a lack of resources and shared experiences for such personal struggles.

After Maddie's passing, Nicole and I made the decision to share our story. Nicole spearheaded an incredible organization called The Maddie Project, aimed at initiating conversations about youth mental health and providing unrestricted access and support for youth and their families. Grief is a strange thing; it can either inspire meaningful change or cripple and halt you in your tracks, preventing you from moving beyond the pain.

I commend Nicole for her impactful work to help others, but, as I've told many people, grief cannot be quantified. There is no expiry date on grieving. Everyone processes grief in their own way, starting with emotional awareness and ending the day they acknowledge it and take steps to work through it. How long is an appropriate time to grieve? Is there a right or wrong answer to this question? It takes however long it takes, and that's alright.

WAKE UP YOU COULD LOSE YOUR TEEN TO SUICIDE

Though Maddie's death happened more than 8.5 years ago, some days it feels like yesterday. The emotion never truly disappears; we just learn to carry it forward on our journey through life.

Sometimes, the weight is too heavy to bear; other times, we sling it over our shoulders, using it to weather through adversity. The most crucial thing is acknowledging, talking about, and finding meaning behind it.

I couldn't engage in the purposeful work that Nicole took on with The Maddie Project so soon after Maddie's death. My path was more organic. I chose to share our story using my voice—the voice of a grieving father. The father's voice often takes a backseat to that of a grieving mother, but for a father, the weight isn't any lighter, the burden any less. For almost every grieving mother, there is a grieving father whose story is seldom told. I'm here to speak for the grieving fathers whose stories haven't been told but need to be told.

In the aftermath of Maddie's passing, I found solace in writing. Uncertain about the topics, I decided to share our journey with Maddie: the pain, the lessons learned, and the grieving process. As I poured my thoughts onto paper and shared them, a stream of messages from parents flooded in—individuals grappling with their private hells concerning their teenagers and young adults.

Hundreds of parents reached out, expressing the value they found in my words. It wasn't because I held all the answers, but rather, they realized they weren't alone. Many faced similar struggles, shared the same questions, and felt lost about where to turn and whom to talk to. Writing became my outlet for grief, a way to navigate the complex emotions surrounding Maddie's death. It also held the potential for some good to emerge from our experiences.

Writing became cathartic for me, an essential part of navigating the grieving process. It unveiled my vulnerabilities as a father, friend, and entrepreneur. While I harboured the desire to extend help on a larger scale, I recognized the necessity of finding comfort within myself and my emotional journey first. As this journey gradually assumed a more predictable course, I could contemplate what lay ahead. Imposing deadlines on oneself in the healing process is counterproductive. Healing doesn't adhere to schedules. I needed time to mend and attempting to hasten the process would only reveal the fragile surface I wasn't ready to expedite.

Chapter 14: What is it Like for a Parent Whose Child is Struggling?

Parenting through the tumultuous teenage years is challenging in itself, and when mental health issues enter the picture, it becomes a battlefield for emotional, marital, and physical well-being. The impact extends beyond the struggling child, affecting parents' mental health, marriages, work, and physical health. Many find themselves in uncharted territory, seeking therapy to cope with the constant worry and isolation that accompanies the journey of supporting a child in crisis.

Our experience with Maddie exposed me to the harsh realities of parenting a child facing mental health challenges. The strain on my emotional well-being was profound, accompanied by a whirlwind of emotions that unfolded in stages.

The Emotional Whirlwind:

After Maddie's first suicide attempt, a storm of shock, disbelief, guilt, and self-doubt engulfed me. The emotional journey as a parent dealing with a child in crisis unfolded like heart-wrenching chapters.

Acknowledging Your Struggles:

One critical realization emerged—dealing with a suffering child is impossible when you're mentally or physically ill-equipped to handle life yourself. Seeking emotional support from therapists, friends, coaches, mentors, or spiritual leaders is crucial. Without this support, you'll be ill-prepared to navigate the challenging road ahead with your child.

The Self-Journey:

Seeing your child go through emotional challenges initiates a profound self-reflection. The journey involves questioning your abilities as a parent and as a human being. There is no scientific backing for my hypothesis, just my own observations from my experiences trying to navigate through an untenable situation with Maddie.

Emotional Stages of Navigating a Parenting Crisis:

1. Denial and Disbelief:

The initial response was rooted in denial—this couldn't be happening to us. Tragedies like this were meant for other families. The challenge lies in the universal vulnerability to mental illness, regardless of background.

2. Shame:

A wave of shame followed, not directed at Maddie but at myself as a parent. Questions about what I had done wrong and whether I was fit to be a parent arose, casting scrutiny on my approach to parenting.

3. **Shield:**

The instinct to insulate Maddie took over, limiting the sharing of our ordeal to a select circle. The plight of a suffering child handcuffs parents, forcing decisions based on instinct rather than a clear thought process.

4. **Fear and Anxiety:**

Fear crept in, fueled by the realization that if Maddie attempted this once, a recurrence was possible. Anxiety set in, manifesting physically with symptoms like insomnia, elevated blood pressure, panic attacks, nausea, sadness and pressure headaches.

5. **Depression:**

The transition from anxiety to depression was swift. Two weeks after Maddie's passing, the anxiety surrounding the fear of losing her lifted, and a heavy cloak of depression settled in. The aftermath, marked by funeral preparations, felt like navigating a turbulent storm of grief.

The Non-Linear Nature of Grieving:

Grieving isn't a linear journey; it's a tumultuous rollercoaster of emotions. The stages of denial, shame, insulation, fear, anxiety, and depression intertwine, creating a complex tapestry of parental grief. Maddie's loss left an indelible mark, and navigating the aftermath meant confronting the depths of despair, each emotion a poignant reminder of the profound impact of mental health struggles on families.

Chapter 15: Does the Sadness Ever Stop?

How do you navigate the first week, month, year, birthdays, and holidays after a loss like Maddie's? You carry on because life insists on moving forward and surrendering to anything less is not an option. I do it for my kids, my family, my friends, and, to some extent, for myself.

In the aftermath of Maddie's passing, I've undergone profound changes. My patience has diminished, and my emotional spectrum can shift from joy to sorrow in about 30 seconds. Reflection has become a constant companion. My focus on self has waned, replaced by a fierce protective instinct for those I love. I've become intolerant of unnecessary challenges and refuse to dwell on trivial matters. The generosity of many has touched me deeply, but there have been disappointments from some I expected more from. I've witnessed the impactful efforts of a few who make a difference in the lives of many. I've seen countless individuals silently grappling with their struggles and crossed paths with those who navigate life just inches above the ground every day. The shame associated with dealing with mental illness is a shared burden.

Everything in my life is now relative to the loss of Maddie.

I understand that few can truly comprehend my world, let alone live inside it. I share a unique bond with a small group of bereaved parents. The weight of our collective grief varies, and while some are immobilized by it, others channel their pain into transformative actions that bring good to the world. Regardless, we are all united by the common thread of pain. Our ability to function and contribute to society is a reflection of how heavy our hearts feel on any given day, balancing the struggle to prevent our sadness from becoming all-consuming.

I've learned that grieving isn't a linear journey but a tumultuous rollercoaster of emotions. Eight years have passed since Maddie's departure, yet the complexity of grief persists for me and many other parents.

Denial and Anger:

Initially, there's an overwhelming disbelief and anger. As a parent, you question yourself, wondering if there was something you could have done differently. It's akin to believing that such tragedies only befall other families, not your own.

Bargaining:

The next stage is marked by bargaining. Deals are made with oneself or a higher power, hoping against hope that circumstances could be different. I vividly recall making countless promises, pleading for a different outcome during Maddie's hospitalization. I've sold my soul numerous times, if only to plead for a different outcome.

Acceptance:

Acceptance arrives sooner than expected, a gradual realization that Maddie is no longer with us. It's a slow-moving phase of the ride, where the understanding dawns that her journey took an unforeseen turn. Acceptance came relatively quickly, likely because I had mentally prepared for the worst scenario months before that fateful day.

Depression:

Depression resembles a roller coaster with unpredictable ups and downs. Some weeks are manageable, while others are immensely challenging. There's no discernible pattern, and it often feels never-ending. Depression is a silent companion that sometimes sits prominently in the front seat and, at other times, resides in the trunk, out of sight but never out of mind. Its appearance lacks predictability, making it an ever-present passenger on this journey.

Alcohol and Mental Health:

The impact of alcohol on one's emotions becomes more pronounced the next day. Even a drink or two can trigger uncontrollable sadness. In response, I decided to temporarily abstain from drinking. It's not a permanent decision, but I recognize that my happiness is better without it. Occasionally, I test how it feels to have a drink, understanding that my relationship with alcohol is delicate. I rarely miss it. I've given up drinking for many months at a time and then easing back into introducing into my life again, being fully aware that the sadness can suddenly appear at any moment.

Eventually, I'll come to the realization that eliminating alcohol from my life altogether is my likely course.

Being completely sober in a social setting sheds light on the complex relationship some people have with alcohol. In my 50s, I've noticed that others' relationships with alcohol can be polarizing—some cut down or eliminate it, while others double down on a predictable path toward self-destruction.

Understanding grief is akin to riding emotional roller coasters and Ferris wheels that defy clear paths. The ups and downs persist but acknowledging that certain feelings might endure is a step toward self-care. The future holds more opportunities for learning and resilience, despite the unpredictable nature of this journey.

Module 4: The Factors

"In the intricate dance of adolescence, each step might not break the rhythm, but the accumulation of missteps can create a haunting melody of struggle."

CHRIS COULTER

Chapter 16: Social Media: The High Price of Likes

Social media acts as a bustling marketplace, a platform where youths showcase their lives to the world, amassing thousands, even tens of thousands, of followers. A single post holds the power to ripple through the lives of countless people. It's a potent force, simultaneously captivating and perilous. But within the realm of followers, how many truly understand the intentions behind their actions?

Participating in social media is like stepping into an arena of scrutiny, vulnerability, and personal attacks. When we share personal stories, we open ourselves to uplifting support and hurtful criticism. Throughout our journey with Maddie, I've been fortunate to receive immense support from friends on Facebook. My LinkedIn blogs have served as a platform to promote my professional endeavours. The power and reach of social media are truly astonishing.

Yet, alongside its positive aspects, social media has a dark side. Some misinterpreted my posts about Maddie, mistakenly thinking I was teetering on the edge of despair. Writing is a form of therapy to gain perspective and find solace. Despite the public scrutiny it invites, I must continue because my blogs have reached many, answering questions, encouraging seeking help, and providing comfort. The benefits of social media far outweigh any scrutiny it may invite.

The combination of social media and its impact on youth profoundly concerns me. To illustrate this point, let me share a recent incident involving a family friend. He regularly confides in me, a testament to his trust in our relationship. However, he is a prime example of why social media is perilous. In a world where likes and followers measure popularity, people allow others into their digital spaces without truly comprehending their intentions.

This young individual has been told by his *"friends"* to end his own life. To make matters worse, several others in their circle liked this cruel comment. The callousness exhibited by some of today's youth is truly unfathomable. Do they even grasp the weight of their words when they put them into writing? How can such behaviour be tolerated in a world that claims to celebrate diversity and inclusion? Regrettably, my young friend is not the only victim, as cyberbullying has driven numerous youths to take their own lives.

A poignant example of the devastating consequences of cyberbullying is the story of Amanda Todd. The burden she carried became so overwhelming that she succumbed to grief and took her own life. In the wake of this tragedy, Amanda's mother, Carol Todd, has dedicated her life to raising awareness about cyberbullying through The Amanda Todd Legacy Society. Carol's work is genuinely remarkable. She speaks at events worldwide and influences public policy. She compels politicians, educators, parents, and youth to reconsider the consequences of their online actions. We must safeguard and preserve the innocence of our youth both in real life and within the digital realm.

In Maddie's case, social media became a significant factor in driving her moods. She would post a picture on Instagram, eagerly awaiting the unbridled reaction of her followers. If likes didn't come at the rate she expected or comments were less complimentary than she would have liked, she would take down the post and reel from the results. Predictably, the success or disappointment of a particular post would be a barometer for her mood. She would brood in her room all day if we let her. This was the reaction of someone who had many friends, was popular, and was never bullied. Imagine if someone like Amanda Todd or my young friend faced that harsh scrutiny every day online. How would you react, or how would your child react?

While social media offers immense connectivity and a platform to express oneself, it also imposes a heavy toll, especially on the fragile minds of adolescents. The relentless pursuit of likes and validation can turn these platforms into battlegrounds where the casualties are often the emotional well-being of our youth. As parents, educators, and society, we need to understand the intricate dynamics of social media and its potential consequences. By fostering a culture of empathy, kindness, and responsible digital citizenship, we can create a safer and more supportive online environment for our children.

Chapter 17: Navigating the Teenage Years: Communication Secrets for Parents

The familiar sight of an eye roll from a teenager during a conversation is a rite of passage for most parents. These interactions often feel like one-way lectures, with teenagers asserting dominance and demanding that parents listen. The Eye Roll Quotient (ERQ) increases as these exchanges become more one-sided. But just as we didn't appreciate such behaviour from our parents, we should question why it would be different for our children. It's time to shift our approach and actively listen to our teens.

Embracing the Uniqueness of Each Teen

Raising teenagers is an immensely challenging task, as each individual is different. Despite our best efforts to seek advice and read books on the subject, we are still trying to prepare for the realities of parenting adolescents. Observing our children, we realize they couldn't be more distinct. What worked with one child may only occasionally yield results with the next. Teenagers constantly change the rules, oscillating between withdrawal and boundary-pushing. It's essential to remember that we are not alone on this journey, and every teenager's parent has felt the same way. While it's undeniably tricky, there are strategies to manage this phase and support our teens.

Parenting with Integrity

Parenting with integrity means leading by example and not asking our teens to do something we are unwilling to do ourselves. Being mindful of our behaviours is crucial, especially when using phones. If we expect our children to stay off their devices during specific times, we should be prepared to follow the same rules. When we hold ourselves to the same standards, we foster a sense of fairness and avoid conflicts that arise from double standards.

Age-Appropriate Risks

Relinquishing control goes against our instinct to be overprotective parents. However, we must grant our children the opportunity to take age-appropriate risks. This may involve allowing them to walk to school with friends at the age of 10, taking the bus independently at 12, or attending their first mixed-gender party at 14. As parents, we determine the appropriateness of each activity based on their age and maturity level. With each metaphorical shackle we loosen, we facilitate their growth and development. Giving independence signals to our children that we trust them to make good decisions, positively impacting their development.

Trying Different Approaches

Raising teenagers involves various concerns, from academics and friendships to dating and social events. Feeling uncertain about the right course of action or the best words is natural. When our initial approaches seem ineffective, persisting with the same approach in a louder or more aggressive manner rarely yields positive results. It's crucial to remember the definition of insanity—trying the same thing repeatedly and expecting a different outcome. Instead, we must be open to trying different approaches, even if it means stepping out of our comfort zones. Persistence, adaptability, and an open mind will eventually lead us to find what works best for our teenagers.

Taking Parent Timeouts

Parenting can be exhausting, with constant arguments, messy bedrooms, and boundary testing. In moments of frustration, it's crucial to give ourselves a timeout. Just as young children benefit from regrouping and calming down, adults sometimes need a few minutes to regain composure. We can prevent saying or doing something we might regret later by taking a timeout. When calmer, we can respond more constructively and respectfully to our teens, fostering a healthier parent-child relationship.

Finding Effective Communication Strategies

Effective communication is a vital aspect of parenting teenagers. It requires understanding, patience, and empathy. Acknowledging that each teenager is unique and may respond differently to various approaches is crucial. Listening actively, without judgment, can create a safe space for open dialogue. Avoiding lecturing or constantly giving advice allows teens to feel heard and respected. Providing gentle guidance, rather than putting excessive pressure on them, allows them the freedom to make mistakes, learn, and grow. By maintaining a positive and supportive attitude, even during challenging times, parents can foster a stronger connection and help their teens navigate the ups and downs of adolescence.

As parents, our ultimate goal is to see our teenagers happy and thriving. To achieve this, we must be willing to adapt our parenting approach, embrace change, and let go of control to some extent. By providing age-appropriate independence, we demonstrate trust in our teens' decision-making abilities and promote their personal growth. Upholding integrity in our parenting, setting a positive example, and fostering effective communication are critical elements in building a solid parent-child relationship during the challenging teenage years. Remember, every teenager is unique, and finding what works best for each individual requires patience, understanding, and a willingness to evolve as parents. Together, let's navigate this journey and support our amazing teens as they navigate adulthood.

Indifference Never Made a Difference

I'm reminded of an incident that tested me, both as a father and as a neighbour. It's also a reminder that being a perfect parent is impossible, primarily because we are subject to flaws as humans. Also, none of us is impervious to mistakes; many variables affect us differently. As a parent, I repeatedly make mistakes and aspire not to repeat them if possible. Choosing to act is a choice we all have and doing nothing isn't one of them; indifference doesn't make a difference.

About two years ago, I moved to a new place. It was an old building that got a makeover and was closer to my youngest son's high school. The walls could have been more soundproof, though. I could hear my neighbours, especially their newborn, who would cry in the middle of the night. It sometimes woke me up, but I'd use my sleeping app and go back to sleep. I figured out they had another child, around three years old.

I remembered those years of having three kids under five, and I understood the stress. I empathized when I heard the father getting loud, saying I didn't miss that parenting stage. The baby cried less at night as time passed, but the father's yelling became more noticeable. I thought being a young parent during a pandemic must be tough. More time passed, and the father's yelling seemed directed at the kids. I wondered if they were going through financial difficulties or if he had lost his job. A couple of weeks ago, I was reading on a Saturday morning when I heard the father screaming at the child, *"Do you want me to hit you again?"* I could no longer be a passive observer. Rationalizing his behaviour made me realize that I couldn't, in good conscience, do nothing.

I thought about my options. I could call the police, but that might be harsh for the family. I could talk to the father, but I was afraid I might lose my temper. Doing nothing was no longer an option.

So, I wrote him a note. I said I was a neighbour and a father of three kids. I knew parenting could be stressful, especially during a pandemic. I didn't know their story, but I couldn't let someone threaten their kid, regardless of how genuine the threat was or wasn't. I mentioned resources for help or offered to talk. I said if I heard a threat again, I would call the police, but I hoped it wouldn't come to that. I quietly slipped the note under their door.

Some might criticize me for not acting earlier or choosing a different way, but I chose empathy and compassion. I offered help and made it clear there would be consequences if it happened again.

Over the following months, I'm happy to report that the only loud noises I heard were laughter, which they can do as much as they want. Parenting is hard. I hope the person interpreted my intrusion as a peace offering, not a threat. His subsequent action has shown me he interpreted my letter as an offer to help. Sometimes, we must be reminded of the importance of our roles as parents.

Chapter 18: Navigating Divorce: Creating a Compassionate Environment for Children

Divorce is undeniably tough, especially for kids. Understanding its impact and ensuring their support is crucial. While controlling emotions in these situations can be challenging, maintaining respect and friendliness with your ex-spouse, especially around your children, can make a significant difference. Reflecting on my divorce, I recognize areas where I could have handled things better; emotions can be overwhelming during these moments.

Fostering a positive co-parenting relationship is essential. Minimizing constant arguing and criticism in front of your kids can enhance their well-being. Remember, you and your ex-spouse chose this path, but your kids didn't. It's crucial to keep them out of your disagreements.

Children should never feel responsible for their parents' split. It's vital to separate personal issues from your role as a parent. Put aside your feelings and concentrate on creating a loving and supportive environment for your child. Avoid using them against your ex-spouse; prioritize their well-being.

Despite the significant changes divorce brings, demonstrating unified support for your child from both parents is possible. Setting aside negative emotions helps in handling challenging situations together. Collaboration becomes crucial when your child faces difficulties, such as illness or emotional struggles. Kids can sense when their parents don't get along and might use it to their advantage—for instance, asking one parent for something and then seeking the same from the other if the first says no. Working together to raise your kids, even post-divorce, is preferable.

Always prioritize your child's needs. They deserve the love of both parents. By placing your child's well-being above all else, you can establish a safe and loving environment for them. Demonstrate ongoing care for their happiness and feelings despite the separation. Divorce doesn't equate to the end of love for your child. Focusing on their needs and collaborating with your ex-spouse can create a positive and stable space for them to grow and thrive. Sometimes, stepping back from an argument is a wiser choice than pushing through to get your way.

Chapter 19: Igniting Your Child's Passion: The Transformative Power of Purposeful Activities

In our fast-paced world, ensuring our kids engage in activities that provide them with purpose and a means to stay active is crucial. It's not limited to sports alone; playing a musical instrument or participating in any focused activity can significantly contribute to their mental well-being.

Recognizing the intensity and uniqueness of each child holds great importance. Take Maddie, for example, a dedicated swimmer training six days a week at a high level. In hindsight, we made a mistake by too quickly agreeing when she expressed a desire to quit. A better approach would have been to adjust her training, perhaps dropping a level or two, while ensuring she continued to enjoy the sport. Exercise, in any form, serves as a fantastic mood booster for everyone.

However, we must be mindful of the potential loss of focus and purpose. Whether it's swimming, gymnastics, hockey, soccer, dance, or cheerleading at a high level, these activities can exert significant pressure on young individuals. The fun can vanish when the stress becomes overwhelming. While listening to our child's desires is crucial, finding a middle ground as parents is equally important.

Balancing our children's aspirations with their overall well-being ensures they continue to find joy in their pursuits. It's not about pushing them too hard but creating an environment where they can derive enjoyment, physical and mental growth, and success.

Remember, engaging our kids in meaningful activities goes beyond merely keeping them occupied. It aids in their development, instils discipline, fosters a sense of accomplishment, and imparts essential life skills. Let's support our kids by allowing them to explore their interests, discover their passions, and comprehend the significance of focus and purpose.

Chapter 20: Unveiling the Hidden Struggles: Nurturing Teen Mental Health with Compassion

As parents, observing shifts in our teenagers' behaviour and wellbeing can be deeply concerning. If, like in Maddie's case, you notice signs such as withdrawing from friends, grappling with self-esteem, and experiencing a lack of motivation, it's crucial to consider the possibility of underlying mental health issues.

Changes in Behaviour and Social Withdrawal:

When your once outgoing and social teenager starts spending extended periods alone, remaining in their room, and loses interest in previously enjoyed activities, it might signal an underlying mental health issue. Engage in open conversations with your teens, creating a safe space for them to express their feelings without judgment.

Impact on Self-Esteem:

Monitor your teen's self-esteem and their perception of their body. If they communicate feeling down, unworthy, or overly critical of themselves, it could indicate a deeper emotional struggle. Reassure them of your love and support and consider seeking professional help if necessary.

Disrupted Eating Patterns:

Significant changes in your teen's appetite, whether an increase or decrease, may indicate emotional distress. Observe their eating habits closely and be prepared to seek advice from healthcare professionals if their relationship with food becomes unhealthy.

Lack of Engagement and Motivation:

If your teen suddenly loses interest in once-enjoyed activities, like spending time with family or pursuing hobbies, it may signal mental health challenges. Encourage them to share their feelings and explore ways to reignite their motivation.

Declining Academic Performance:

A decline in your teen's grades without an apparent reason could be a sign of emotional distress affecting their focus. Provide educational support and collaborate with teachers or school counsellors to effectively address the issue.

Mood Swings and Energy Levels:

Fluctuating moods, persistent lows, or consistently low energy levels can lead to emotional struggles. Encourage your teens to express their emotions freely, validate their experiences, and make them aware that professional help is available.

Recognizing these signs of mental health issues in teenagers, akin to the changes in Maddie's behaviour, is a crucial step in guiding them toward well-being. By maintaining open communication, seeking professional guidance as needed, and fostering a caring environment, you can support your teen in navigating these challenges and finding the assistance they require. Remember, you're not alone in this journey; seeking help reflects your strength and concern for your teenager's mental health.

Chapter 21: Navigating a Journey of Trust in Communication

Parents often feel pressure to have all the answers for their children, but its fine to admit that we don't know everything. Understanding our limits can help build trust with our kids and lead to more meaningful conversations. Showing our vulnerability creates a space where both parent and child can explore and discover answers, promoting growth and understanding.

It's important to realize that nobody likes someone who acts like they know everything, and our kids are no different. Pretending to have all the answers can create a barrier between us and our children, making them think we're perfect and know everything. This can be intimidating and stop open communication. Instead, when we admit we don't have all the answers, we show humility and authenticity, making way for real connections and more profound talks.

Acknowledging our limits opens the door for teamwork and shared learning. Exploring knowledge together with our children encourages their curiosity and helps them develop critical thinking and problem-solving skills. By approaching discussions with curiosity, we invite our kids to actively join in finding answers, empowering them to take charge of their learning and growth.

Moreover, saying we don't have all the answers sets a good example for our children. It teaches them that asking questions, seeking help, and admitting when they don't know something is perfectly okay. By embracing our vulnerability, we encourage our kids to be vulnerable, creating a trusting and understanding atmosphere in the parent-child relationship.

It's essential to remember that admitting we don't know everything doesn't make us less of a parent. It makes us stronger. By being honest about our limits, we show that we are human, just like our children, and we are always learning and growing with them. This vulnerability deepens the connection between parent and child, showing we're willing to grow and adapt.

In moments when we don't have the answers, we can turn it into a chance for connection and growth. Have conversations that encourage thinking, curiosity, and a shared quest for knowledge. We create an atmosphere of respect and teamwork by actively listening to our children's thoughts and letting them share their insights.

So, let go of the pressure to have all the answers. Embrace the beauty of vulnerability and the potential for growth in your parent-child relationship. Together, you can go on a journey of discovery, learning, and meaningful conversations that will build trust, deepen understanding, and foster a lifelong love of learning. Remember, admitting you don't have all the answers is totally okay.

Chapter 22: Embarking on the Journey to Emotional Freedom

Feelings play a significant role in how we think and feel. Understanding this can help our mental and emotional health. I've learned that dealing with feelings healthily is important, and I want to share this lesson, especially with younger parents.

Holding in your feelings is like carrying a heavy load. Many people do it without realizing how much it can affect their mental and emotional well-being. I went through this, too, thinking that if I ignored my feelings, they would go away. But they didn't. Instead, they turned into problems like trouble sleeping, anger, stress, and anxiety. Ignoring emotions can be harsh on us and our relationships. While putting some feelings aside for a bit is okay, it's not a good long-term solution.

Expressing emotions is like a healing superpower. It might feel uncomfortable initially, but it's worth it for the relief afterward. Understanding our feelings helps release built-up stress and tension, giving us a sense of freedom and better well-being.

As parents, we must guide our kids in dealing with their emotions, so they don't face the same struggles. Talking openly about feelings, teaching healthy coping methods, and being ready to get help are important steps in their emotional growth.

It's also okay to admit that we might not fully understand emotional intelligence. Sometimes, letting someone else teach our kids about understanding and expressing their emotions is better.

Talking openly:

Start honest conversations about your feelings and encourage your kids to do the same. I'm still learning how to express my emotions in a healthy way, and its okay to keep learning.

Healthy coping:

Give your kids tools to deal with emotions early on, like writing in a journal, talking to someone, exercising, or doing creative things. Having different ways to handle emotions helps them navigate feelings positively.

Getting help:

Don't ignore signs that your kids might be holding in their emotions. If needed, contact professionals like therapists specializing in child and teen psychology. This proactive approach helps address issues early and lets your kids develop important emotional skills.

Leading by example is a powerful way to guide our kids. Showing them healthy ways to cope and being open about our struggles teaches them the value of expressing emotions and seeking help. When we create a safe space for them to share their feelings, it builds trust and makes our parent-child relationship stronger.

Breaking the cycle of holding in emotions is essential. By raising awareness of how it can harm us, we can consciously work against this habit for our mental health and as a positive example for our kids. Showing them the importance of dealing with emotions and giving them the tools helps them embrace and healthily handle their feelings. Let's break the cycle of holding in emotions and create a supportive environment for our well-being and the wellbeing of future generations. Through my work with How Are You Feeling, a non-profit that teaches kids about emotions, I've seen a positive impact on students' understanding of their emotions. It helps them avoid holding in or avoiding their feelings. I'll explore more resources for parents and teens in the final module.

Chapter 23: The Pressures of Being a Teenager Today

Being a teenager, these days seem tough, and I wouldn't want to go through it willingly. Parenting was never easy, but now, with social media, tons of technology, and our kids knowing more than us in some areas, being a parent is far more complicated.

Life used to be simpler, a feeling passed down through generations that our tech-savvy kids might not get. But things are moving fast now, not just between generations but even from the oldest to the youngest child. How many more things will change when our kids become parents?

Looking back, I got my first cell phone at 21, and it was this big thing you had to mount in the car. Making a call on it costs a small fortune. Now, I see eight or 9-year-olds with fancy smartphones. The change happened so quickly; five or six years ago, getting your first cell phone was a big deal in high school. The disappearance of home phones might be part of this quick change.

In the 80s, organizing house parties meant calling on the *"home phone"* to make plans. Parties could get a bit wild, but it was limited. Now, parents letting their kids have parties step into uncertain territory. Even with security measures, a small event can become a big deal online in minutes. I picked up my daughter from a party once, and there were as many kids outside trying to get in as inside, and the parents were home!

In my youth, we didn't talk about mental health except for whispers about eating disorders or suicide attempts. Now, teenage mental health struggles are common and tragic events spread like wildfire. Likes on social media can impact a teenager's self-esteem, and once something is out there, it's out there forever. Smartphones make everyone a paparazzo, documenting every moment. Mistakes, once forgiven and forgotten, can now haunt a teenager forever.

In my youth, learning from mistakes meant growing personally and being self-aware. There's no tolerance for any mistake, with public humiliation becoming normal. The flow of information among kids is crazy. Last week, my son heard about events in Europe and immediately texted his friend in the affected city. Within seconds, he learned her family was safe but uncomfortably close to the tragedy.

Even though our kids love their devices, they aren't immune to the pain caused by social media. My daughter's mood changing based on Instagram likes isn't a one-time thing. Parents talk about how their kids get upset because of mean comments or bad posts.

Our kids are growing up too fast, and while progress is good, it also brings a tough reality. The most important lessons our kids learn might happen on social media, and they might never fully recover. It's a tough situation that needs our understanding, empathy, and acknowledgment that being a teenager today is a journey we wouldn't wish on ourselves.

Module 5: The Future

"Beyond the numbers lies a pressing challenge: to empower our teens with the tools to navigate their emotional landscapes before the storm hits. Prevention is the key to rewriting their mental health narrative."

Chapter 24: Prevention Versus Remediation?

The future of youth mental health and understanding emotional health is fundamental to our kids navigating this emotional storm. In February 2023, the Centre for Disease Control came out with this shocking statistic: 60% of teenage females have dealt with crippling depression or anxiety. Thirty percent of boys in the same group experienced the same challenges. That means 40% of all teens have experienced crippling and severe depressive issues. Sadly, 30% have contemplated suicide. For years, we had been told one in five teens (20%) would experience mental health challenges. The revised numbers are of epidemic proportions.

The challenge is ensuring these kids are taught to recognize, understand and process their complex emotions before they're in crisis. While they're in crisis, preventative strategies are of no consequence.

It's always been said prevention dollars go much further than remediation dollars. Prevention gets heralded as the long-term answer, yet remediation gets all the money and attention. Very few people pick up a self-help book unless you're going through something. Physical health and mental health are tied to this premise. Who's inclined to act: the guy who's one hundred pounds overweight or the guy who's one hundred pounds overweight and just had a heart attack?

Being involved with a not-for-profit called How Are You Feeling? Has given me a unique perspective on youth mental health. The program aims to teach kids about emotional awareness, using segments from TV and movies to discuss the importance of understanding emotions. As someone who volunteered as an advisor and later became the executive director, my journey has shed light on the lack of programs available for today's youth to grasp their emotions, especially when dealing with complex feelings like grief.

The program, built around popular TV and movie segments, incorporates narration to provide context. It's been my first step into supporting youth mental health, but it has highlighted the challenges of actively engaging schools. We initially focused on private schools, thinking they might be more agile and accountable, less entangled in the bureaucracy than public schools. However, this assumption was naive.

Despite their claims of having a mental health focus, private schools were not significantly better than public schools. The emphasis on mental health often seemed geared towards appeasing parents paying substantial tuition fees. Administrators often ignored our attempts to involve private schools in focus groups. It became clear that we needed a different approach.

WAKE UP YOU COULD LOSE YOUR TEEN TO SUICIDE

We decided to leverage the mandatory volunteer hour program, a graduation requirement for all Ontario high school students. This program required at least 40 volunteer hours, and some private schools mandated as many as 80 hours. Coming out of the challenges posed by COVID-19, volunteer opportunities were limited, making our program a valuable option. The program involved watching 12 hours of content and participating in four moderated online sessions. We encouraged students to recruit their friends, and our calls typically had 10-15 participants each.

The interaction on our calls was remarkable. Not only did the students love the program, but they also became advocates, promoting it within their schools. Beyond their enthusiasm, we received insightful feedback, helping us identify areas for improvement. A crucial statistic was that 97% of participants felt more equipped to handle a crisis after completing the program.

Despite students' positive feedback and endorsements, I was disheartened by the schools' indifference. Even in the face of alarming teenage mental health statistics, many schools chose not to engage with us. Over 500 students underwent the volunteer program, boasting a 94% acceptance rate. Astonishingly, 96% of students felt that what they were learning about emotional health in their schools was insufficient and unsustainable.

Despite positive results and the pressing need for mental health education, this lack of interest from schools discouraged me. The program's impact on students was clear, yet the educational institutions seemed hesitant to embrace the opportunity. The stark reality of the indifference towards youth mental health in the education system was disheartening.

The program forged ahead in the face of these challenges, positively impacting the students who participated. It became a testament to the resilience and determination of those committed to improving youth mental health, even in the face of institutional inertia. The journey continues, and the hope remains that more schools will recognize the importance of emotional well-being education for their students.

Government alone won't bring the meaningful change we need in mental health. While there's a Minister of Mental Health, the real transformation must start on a broader scale. People often talk about the mental health crisis, but it's challenging to make significant changes in a government filled with party politics. Natalie Pierre, MPP from Burlington, Ontario, faced the heartbreaking loss of her son to suicide in 2017. In 2022, she ran for a seat in the provincial government to improve the education system.

Earlier this year, a bill was passed to introduce mental health education into grade 10 classrooms. Additional resources will be available for grades seven and eight. The question lingers: will we witness substantial change in the next five years? It's hard to say. Unfortunately, while seeking the greater good, many politicians get entangled in political partisanship, lobby and interest groups, and re-election concerns. This often leads elected officials to toe the party line or become permanent backbenchers. Was I too hopeful that politics wouldn't overpower the real issues in government?

Our schools crave strong leadership that prioritizes students over pensions and the fear of consequences. It's intriguing that the How Are You Feeling program found a welcoming home in a multicampus school in Portugal and Spain. This school stands out by emphasizing individual expression and learning. Unconventional schools like these are more open-minded, recognizing the importance of self-expression and integrating emotional well-being with academic pursuits.

Interestingly, many private schools in Canada focus on elevated learning to secure coveted spots in universities. However, the irony is that academic success cannot happen without emotional health. It's a universal truth whether you attended a private or public school. Reflecting on my university peers, the private school students were just as challenged emotionally as their public-school counterparts.

Chapter 25: Greater Emphasis on Teaching Emotional Intelligence

Why isn't emotional intelligence (EI) at the forefront of our educational system when it's deemed crucial for success? A report from Mental Health Research Canada revealed that the EI of today's youth is at the same level as it was 30 years ago. This seems perplexing, given that studies consistently highlight EI as a more significant predictor of success than IQ. So, why aren't we prioritizing this essential skill in our schools?

Our schools need to focus intensely on developing emotional intelligence in our children. This critical life skill involves being aware of and understanding one's emotions and the emotions of others. Yet, it is given secondary importance in our education system.

Here are three compelling reasons why emotional intelligence is crucial for our kids:

Developing Self-Awareness:

Emotionally intelligent kids can recognize and understand their emotions, leading to better self-management. This not only promotes improved mental health but also enhances overall wellbeing.

Building Positive Relationships:

Emotional intelligence equips kids to relate better to others, fostering healthy and positive relationships. This skill is fundamental for their social and emotional development.

Coping with Stress and Adversity:

Kids with emotional intelligence possess the tools to navigate stressful situations, fostering resilience and emotional stability.

If emotional intelligence is an invaluable skill for our children, why don't we ensure they develop it early? We can kick start this process by helping them become aware of their emotions, name their feelings, and recognize emotional attachments.

Identifying emotional attachments is a critical aspect of EI. By understanding how emotions influence behaviour, kids can learn coping strategies, such as processing emotions as they occur, practicing deep breathing, and engaging in positive self-talk.

The Importance of Self-Awareness:

Self-awareness, another crucial life skill, involves being conscious of one's thoughts, feelings, and actions and understanding how they impact others. It requires regulating emotions, setting boundaries, and managing stress. Teaching self-awareness to our kids will help them become well-rounded adults capable of confidently navigating life's challenges.

How to Manage Our Emotions:

Emotions are a normal and healthy part of our lives, but sometimes they can overwhelm us. Practical tools for managing emotions include labelling, regulating breathing, and expressing ourselves healthily. By understanding and addressing our emotions constructively, we can maintain emotional well-being.

Improving Relationships Through EI

To enhance relationships through emotional intelligence, one must learn to regulate emotions, read other people's emotions, and create positive connections. Relationships can thrive by managing feelings, interpreting others' emotions, and fostering empathy and effective communication.

Our schools must prioritize emotional intelligence to cultivate emotionally intelligent and successful adults. The foundation of emotional awareness is crucial for our kids' understanding and development of emotional intelligence, setting them up for a successful and fulfilling future. Would we be facing the same mental health crisis amongst our teens today if greater emphasis was placed on understanding emotional intelligence in our schools? Yes, the answer is rhetorical.

Choosing to be an activist and speak out about something as painful as the loss of a loved one to mental health struggles is a profoundly personal decision, one that comes with a mix of emotions. After 8 1/2 years, some details may fade, but the vivid memories remain as if etched into my heart yesterday. Writing a book about such a journey stirs up raw emotions, unearths details never shared before, and sometimes brings tears.

Sharing these intimate details can be a painful yet cathartic experience. It connects me more deeply with Maddie, bringing back the pain of loss and the vibrant memories of her laughter and humour. Despite the resurgence of pain, I choose not to mute these memories. For me, the pain is a small price to pay for the richness of Maddie's memory.

Chapter 26: To Be an Activist or Not?

My decision to be an activist stem from a desire to share my experience and offer solace to others navigating similar storms. It's a testament to the kindness I've encountered along my journey—a journey I've chosen to open up to those who might not know where to turn. Messages from those who've read my story, acknowledging my loss or seeking guidance for their struggles, serve as a reminder of the impact sharing can have.

Connecting with other parents who share this unimaginable loss forms a part of an exclusive and unwanted society—the "F*&$king Awful Club." It's a club no one wishes to join, but through sharing experiences, I hope to create a space where others find solace and understanding. The decision to share doesn't impose an obligation on everyone; it's a personal choice. I hope that, by speaking openly about our loss, I pave the way for others to share their stories and, in turn, support more families.

Reflecting on my journey, I wished for greater transparency during the darkest times, but Maddie's well-being was always the primary consideration. The progress in discussing mental illness is acknowledged, yet there's a recognition that the journey toward openness is ongoing. The stigma persists, and my hope is for a future where mental illness is discussed as openly as physical ailments, devoid of judgment and cruelty.

WAKE UP YOU COULD LOSE YOUR TEEN TO SUICIDE

In my advocacy, I envision a world where mental health discussions are as commonplace as conversations about cancer or a broken arm. It's a vision fueled by the belief that openness can bring about change, create understanding, and, ultimately, save lives.

Chapter 27: Creating Resources for Parents

Today's biggest challenge is the shortage of resources for parents seeking help. Navigating the healthcare system when your child is in crisis is painful and disheartening. I aim to create the most extensive mental health resource directory for families seeking help for a loved one. The last part of this book will be dedicated to available resources, aiming to expand and become a valuable tool for families outside Toronto, Canada.

Here's where the power of community comes in. A community that steps up, as people have stepped up to help my family. You might not realize you need help today, but you or your child might be in need tomorrow, and you won't know where to turn. If you want to help, I plan to update a PDF accessed by an outside portal. All I need is someone to act as the conduit for a province or region. No one should be denied access because they don't know where to go.

Advocacy and strategic thinking can give hope and access to mental health resources for families that need them. You can email me at WakeUpResourceGuide@gmail.com. Let's make this an unforgettable community!

Email me outlining the province or region you live in and whether you'd prefer to help coordinate your mental health resource directory or if you'd like to recommend some mental health practitioners for your area.

WakeUpResourceGuide@gmail.com

Include the following information if recommending a resource:

- *Name of Practitioner or Service*
- *Website*
- *Contact info: Name of Contact, email, phone, address*
- *Service provided: Social worker, psychotherapists, Psychologist, Psychiatrist etc.*
- *Specialty: Depression Anxiety, ADHD, Addiction, Shelter, Eating Disorders etc.*
- *Online/In Person*

Chapter 28: What Are Your 13 Reasons to Thrive?

Watching "*13 Reasons Why*," a series delving into teenage struggles, was a challenging journey for me. Despite warnings, I was drawn into its themes of bullying and mental health. The raw portrayal hit close to home, resonating with the ripple effects of Maddie's tragic story in our North Toronto community.

Our family's story, known to many, spreads through social circles and media. Maddie's tale is crucial—it dispels the myth that these struggles only happen to others. Looking to the future, we must guide our teens towards promise, giving them reasons to live rather than excuses not to.

I, too, faced grief and depression. Some days were a struggle, questioning life's worth. In these moments, my list of reasons to live kept me going. It steadied my ship and brought everything back to the centre.

Laughter as a Lifeline:

When things got tough, I found comfort in laughter. It's like a superpower that can make even the heavy stuff feel lighter. Remembering how Maddie used to laugh helped me see that finding joy, even in hard times, is crucial.

Learning Through Adversity:

Starting a new business when I was feeling lost taught me a lot. I appreciated how tough times can help us grow. Even when it seemed impossible, I discovered a strength in myself that kept me going. This journey also helped me better understand what my kids go through in school, making me want to support them even more.

Sunshine and Mood:

I learned that sunshine could affect how we feel. It's not just about the weather; it's like a mood booster. Feeling the warmth of the sun on a nice day reminded me that even in dark times, there's a promise that things will get better.

Exercise for the Mind and Body:

Moving my body every day became a game-changer. Whether it's a walk or a workout, it greatly helps my mood. Listening to an audiobook or podcast while exercising became my way to stay positive and deal with challenges.

Gratitude as the Foundation:

Believing in the good things, even small ones, became the basis of my journey. It made me realize that no matter how hard things get, there's always something to be grateful for. It's like a secret power that makes each day count.

Friendship:

Real friends are like a safety net. It's not about having lots of them; it's about having deep connections. They've supported me, giving me a shoulder to lean on when things got tough.

The Healing Power of Love:

Getting love from family and friends is like a healing potion. Their support and warmth healed my broken heart. A simple gesture or a kind word reminded me that I'm not alone on this journey.

Beyond Personal Loss:

Maddie's loss opened my eyes to others going through hard times. People like Carol Todd, Eric Windeler, Nicole German, and Zac and Sawyer Coulter turned their pain into something positive. Their stories inspired me to find ways to help others.

Melodies of Life:

Music is like a magic spell that can make you feel different things. It can make you happy or help you when you're sad. It's a source of comfort, motivation, and connection.

Embracing the Future:

Thinking about the future became my motivation. I imagine personal and collective growth and dreams coming true. Seeing my loved ones achieve milestones keeps me going. I want to leave something good for the next generations.

Love:

Love is like an endless source inside us. It gives us purpose and helps us understand others. Love lets us face tough times and celebrate the good moments together.

Family:

Family is like a rock that never moves. They're there through thick and thin, providing comfort and strength. They teach us important values and shape who we are. In sad times, the family becomes a safe place to remember and honour those we've lost.

The Spirit of Sport:

Sports are more than just games; they're exciting and bring people together. Whether you're playing or cheering for your team, sports unite us in the thrill of competition and victory.

As I look back, inspired by the themes in *"13 Reasons Why,"* these life lessons—laughter, learning, sunshine, exercise, gratitude, friendship, love, making a difference, music, embracing the future, family bonds, and the spirit of sport—show the strength in all of us. They guide me to appreciate the good things, face challenges, and leave a legacy of love and kindness.

"What are your 13 Reasons to Thrive?"

CHRIS COULTER

Module 6: The Reflection

"Parenting is the constant dance between reflection and action, where wisdom is born in the pauses between steps."

Chapter 29: Time Gives Us the Ability to Reflect

8 ½ years. 95 months. 448 weeks. 3,150 days. 75,350 hours. 4,530,000 minutes. 271,215,000 seconds. That's the time that has passed since we lost Maddie to suicide. Time feels different when you pour your heart into an event. April 10th, 2015, is a date etched in my heart, more than the birth of my three children or any world-changing event. The hour leading up to midnight on April 11, 2015, freezes time. Maddie was born on June 28, 2000, and officially passed on April 11, 2015, but I remember the moment I felt her go. That's why I always acknowledge April 10th as the saddest day of my life. Milestones like birthdays, Father's Day, Christmas, Thanksgiving, and vacations are marked by an asterisk. My joy will never be as complete. There's always a pause on these days, thinking about how much richer they would've been with Maddie here.

Grief is a peculiar journey. It's unpredictable, and the emptiness inside is indescribable. I've considered joining Maddie several times, but my love for my boys prevents me from seriously considering it. You ponder ways to ensure Maddie's death wasn't in vain. Ending my life might be easy, but I'd rather face a thousand struggles, wondering what could've been done differently. I'm sure I've been challenged to love since then. Dating someone with depression isn't easy. No one can compete for the love I had for Maddie. I've been in wonderful relationships with amazing women but might have unintentionally sabotaged them. I get dark and go inward, making communication challenging at times. I suddenly changed course. I've used my depression and grief as an excuse to end a relationship. Is this dysfunctional? Perhaps, but sometimes I just want to feel miserable. I'm trying to be a better partner, but it's taken me a long time to find the right person or be right in my head. I'll have to be content living my life one happy day at a time.

On one particular April 11th, a friend suggested I talk to a spiritualist who could connect me with Maddie. I've never been a believer in connecting with spirits, thinking palm readers and psychics were for those who couldn't find closure or were desperate. I was a bit of both. I visited a spiritual advisor, not sure if that was her official title, who attempted to connect me to Maddie's spirit. This was unlike the pragmatic person I thought I was. "Lynn" tried to connect me to Maddie but said she was scared or unwilling to talk directly to me. I left feeling unfulfilled, thinking I got hosed out of $200. On some level, you believe what you want to believe.

In the past, I believed I received signs from Maddie in the form of a little bunny. I'd sit in the backyard, and this bunny would lie under a cherry tree about 15 feet from me. I wanted to believe it was Maddie, convincing myself it was her. The bunny would appear on walks, stop, and stare at me. I'd have conversations with my little friend, imagining what it would be like today if Maddie were here.

There are moments when I find myself contemplating things, I wish I had handled them differently, regretting both the words I spoke and the ones I failed to. Has my approach to parenting transformed with Sawyer and Zac? I'm more aware of our conversations and their potential impact. I'm a better listener, more protective, and mindful of my reactions during our interactions.

I often wonder what I would say to Maddie if she were here today.

Some mornings, I wake from dreams where Maddie and I have heartfelt conversations. The origin of these dreams is uncertain, and they sometimes feel vividly real. The subconscious mind can be cruel and hopeful in how it toys with our emotions and grief. Sadly, these dreams never last long enough, and I'm left yearning for their continuation, aware they must end.

In the wake of everything that has happened, what would a conversation with Maddie look like today? Would remorse permeate our exchange? Could anything have altered the outcome? Was I a good father?

The bond between Maddie and me was anything but predictable and far from perfect. We had moments typical of fathers and teenage daughters, where humour provided relief amid tense conversations. However, it sometimes became a source of strain. I didn't always grasp the challenges Maddie faced as a teenage girl. It wasn't a lack of sympathy but a failure to fully comprehend her experiences.

Maddie held a unique place as our first child and the only girl. From the moment she entered my world, she claimed my heart. The birth of Zac didn't diminish my love for her; it expanded it.

"So, Dad, how are the boys doing?"

"They speak of you as if you were still here. Zac even moved into your room, wanting a closer connection. Sawyer is filled with inquiries. Holidays are the most challenging; we keenly feel your absence."

"How is Mom?"

"She has good and bad days. Your absence created a profound void, but she strives to preserve your memory positively. The Maddie Project has had a significant impact, providing some comfort. Your brothers and friends embraced the cause. Your absence created a void but birthed profound goodness. I know you'd be proud."

"And how are you doing, Daddy?"

"I miss you more than words can express. I long for answers. Could we have prevented the path you chose? Songs by Jason Mraz or Ed Sheeran brings tears to my eyes. There's a profound emptiness. Watching your friends grow reminds me of all the experiences you'll never have."

WAKE UP YOU COULD LOSE YOUR TEEN TO SUICIDE

"Tell me, Mads, is your pain gone now?"

"I miss you every day. Leaving you all was agonizing, but I couldn't bear to subject you to my pain. I hope you'll understand. I'm in a better place now."

"Daddy, will you stay with me?"

"I'll stay as long as I can. I wish I could stay indefinitely, but there are responsibilities. We carry you in our hearts every day. Farewell, my Baby Girl. You're loved beyond measure."

I wake up, and for a moment, I smile at the prospect that I have just had a visit with my girl. I rarely remember my dreams, but dreams about Maddie are vivid and realistic. Our subconscious can be so cruel, yet kind.

Chapter 30: How Children Navigate the Sudden Loss of a Sibling

As much as this story is primarily about Maddie, my sons, Sawyer and Zac, have been unbelievable throughout the entire experience, before, during and then in the wake of Maddie's passing. These boys have been nothing short of incredible. How a nine and thirteen-year-old navigates through this storm of emotion is beyond my comprehension. Most kids, if put in the position to spend hours in a hospital for months on end without a single complaint, are unimaginable. Only maturity, empathy, and compassion will teach you always to smile, constantly engage, and put your sister's needs ahead of theirs.

After Maddie's passing, both boys wanted to be involved in spreading the message about the importance of being a good friend and watching out for one another. Zac wanted to do this as a tribute and honour to his sister. Zac spoke from his heart to thousands of kids across the city. Nothing makes a parent prouder than when your children unselfishly put someone else's needs above their own. Sawyer, although much younger, continues to support mental health initiatives. Both have been actively involved since Maddie died and continue to speak and raise money today.

Are my boys superhuman? Yeah, they are incredible examples for others. They've been forced to grow up far too quickly and deal with situations that anyone would be challenged to handle. They truly are my heroes.

I'm reminded that my boys are victims in their own right. They have their sad days, you would expect. We visit Maddie at Mount Pleasant Cemetery, reflect upon our shared memories and recall stories that make us all laugh. Maddie was a character to anyone who knew her. No one knew this more than her brothers.

Not everyone can manage the death of a sibling like these sacred souls. While sharing Maddie's story, we met many individuals who faced pain and devastation. These encounters become therapeutic, where we exchange stories, emotions, and support. Though different in outcomes, these tales share a common thread of pain, emotion, and the courage to share despite discomfort.

During a hockey fundraiser for Sawyer's team, I connected with parents who became invaluable to my support network. One introduction stood out. A woman, moved by reading one of my blogs, teared up when we spoke. This empathetic response, not the first time, always leaves an impact. We talked, and I offered comfort. The following day, she emailed, apologizing and sharing her emotions. Her pain wasn't just that of a parent; it was empathy for Zac and Sawyer, envisioning their challenges. She tragically lost her teenage brother over two decades ago, and the pain lingers. Her message reminded me to ensure my boys receive ongoing support.

As parents, we question if we're doing everything to help our boys navigate the loss of Maddie. Some behaviours stem from her loss, while others are part of being boys. We maintain open communication and a deep bond. They've had counselling, and we actively seek ways to alleviate their pain. They participate in fundraisers and support The Maddie Project.

Six local high schools chose The Maddie Project as the charity of the year. Zac, especially, volunteered as The Maddie Project Ambassador. Stepping outside his comfort zone, he'll speak at assemblies, combating the stigma of teenage mental illness from a personal perspective as Maddie's brother.

Knowing Zac means understanding that stepping outside his comfort zone is difficult. Driven by his passion for the cause and profound empathy, he recognizes the importance of conveying this message. Zac, with his compassionate and caring nature, does not want another brother or sister to endure the profound sadness and loss that he and Sawyer have experienced through the loss of their sister. The high schools could not have made a better choice in selecting him.

Chapter 31: From Siblings to Pillars: The Impact of Loss on Family Dynamics

The impact of losing Maddie has woven a unique spin into the relationship between Zac, Sawyer, and me. The strong and interconnected bond that Maddie shared with her brothers naturally extended to envelop our entire family. The sudden loss of their sister undeniably left an indelible mark on Zac and Sawyer's lives, altering the course of their journey in profound ways. Yet, despite the weight of this tragedy, their strength and support have been nothing short of extraordinary.

As a parent, navigating the complexities of grief while supporting the emotional needs of two boys presented its own set of challenges. Boys, often less communicative about their emotions than girls, tend to deflect attention from themselves. The inclination to worry about me worrying about them creates an additional layer of complexity. It requires a delicate balance of pushing through typical responses like *"I'm fine"* and delving deeper to uncover potential underlying issues.

Our shared experiences, especially during the times spent going to and from the hockey arena, became the canvas on which our bond deepened. While grand gestures may have been beyond our means, the decision to spend quality time together proved to be an invaluable choice. With both boys now at university, the dynamics of our interactions have evolved, but the foundation of our closeness remains intact.

Zac, with his calm and stoic demeanour, exudes a laissez-faire attitude that brings a sense of calmness to those around him. There's a natural tendency to worry less about him, as his quiet confidence becomes a source of reassurance. Sawyer, on the other hand, is more animated and high-strung, commanding attention with his vibrant energy. Both boys, despite their differences, embody leadership qualities in their distinct ways.

Our shared stories about Maddie, her antics, and the memories we hold dear continue to be a thread that ties us together. While distance may pose challenges to our physical togetherness, the stories we share, like our golf round on Father's Day, serve as bridges that connect us across the miles. The laughter that accompanies these shared memories becomes a form of catharsis, a way to navigate the complexities of grief and find moments of joy in sorrow.

Father's Day, in particular, carries profound reflections on the impact of Maddie's presence in our lives. Countless voices have chronicled her journey, emphasizing her remarkable qualities — unwavering strength, infectious humour, boundless love, tireless support, steadfast loyalty, and deep compassion for others. While the narrative often focuses on Maddie's journey, the contribution of her brothers to this story often remains in the background.

As laughter and camaraderie filled the air, anecdotes about Maddie naturally found their way into our conversations. Each reminiscence served as a gentle reminder that, while we cherished the moments shared as a threesome, only one person could adequately round out our group. The physical absence of Maddie tugged at our hearts, but her essence resonated with every step we took on the golf course.

The unspoken understanding that she was, and will always be, an integral part of our lives permeated the air. The golf outing became more than a recreational activity; it became a poignant journey through memories and reflections. The impact of Maddie's absence was juxtaposed with the enduring love and support displayed by Zac and Sawyer throughout the arduous journey.

Our foursome, though forever incomplete without her, carries forward the spirit of Maddie in every shared story, every laughter-filled moment, and every step we take on this journey of healing. As we concluded our golf outing, the immense gratitude I felt for the unwavering love and support of my sons, Zac and Sawyer, was immeasurable. Together, we have forged an unbreakable bond fueled by the memories of Maddie and the indomitable spirit she embodied. Our lives may carry the ache of her absence, but her memory now brings smiles of remembrance, not tears of sorrow.

Needless to say, upon embarking on this journey and deciding to capture what we went through with Maddie, I wouldn't have gone down this road without the unconditional support, love and influence of both boys on this story. Respectfully, they were the first ones to read this book. I wanted to ensure this wasn't too personal or too triggering for them. Although they both acknowledged it was tough to read and sad in places, they confirmed that it was a story too important not to share.

Chapter 32: How I Will Choose to Remember Maddie

My words about Maddie often come from our experiences about six months before she left us. I've covered strategies for parents to learn from our loss, its impact on our family and friends, the awareness it has brought, and some of my innermost thoughts, feelings, and emotions that people often ask me about.

The focus has been on awareness and prevention for over eight and a half years. But not enough attention has been given to the life Maddie lived for the majority of her almost fifteen years. The real legacy of Maddie Coulter should be about the incredible person she was, not just the kid who ended her life so suddenly. These fading details are what I want to cherish and honour my daughter's memory with. Despite all the good achieved in Maddie's loss, it would be lost upon us if we didn't acknowledge the life she lived, the person she was, and the lives she touched along the way. Here are some things I miss most about Maddie:

-The massive collection of girl's shoes and boots at the front door, sometimes making it challenging to open the door.

-Maddie's constant requests to clean her room, even though she'd mostly ignore my pleas. When she did clean it, she'd proudly show me, even though I knew she shoved most of the clutter in her closet or under her bed.

-Special requests for items to add to our grocery lists, like quinoa, kale, special shampoos, conditioners, face masks and bubble bath salts.

-Shouts from her bedroom after posting something on Instagram, asking me to *"Like my picture!"*

-Her singing Adele loudly in the shower.

-Goofy Snapchat photos she'd want me to pose for while driving or the constant selfies she took.

-Comments about my wardrobe claims that we weren't living in the 1980s, or critiques of my gift-giving abilities.

-Sitting with me while browsing online dating profiles and giving thumbs up or down (though very few got her approval).

-Watching classic movies together, with her letting me choose (our favourite was Stand By Me).

-Trips to eat at Freshii or the Sushi Shoppe.

-Her sensitivity and empathy when I had a tough week, giving me a big hug and saying, *"I love you, Daddy."*

-her ruckus laughs, bold character, and outrageous side that could shake a house and light up a room when she was in it.

-her bossing Zac and Sawyer around and the boys accepting it. She automatically held the shotgun position in the car, and the boys didn't dispute it. She'd let Zac sit in the front seat only on Wednesday mornings.

-her absolute love of music, reciting every lyric from every song and singing unabashedly.

-how she started a One Direction fan club on Twitter, gaining over 1,500 followers within a few weeks.

-her intensity, focus, and self-motivation before every swim meet or race.

-her non-conforming and individualistic nature. She only did what she wanted. She left Camp Wapamao because too many friends started going, and there was too much drama.

- All the videos she'd create within PhotoBooth.

-E-Mad and the comedy skits she and her cousin Emma would perform at the cottage.

-how Maddie and Emma could make my mom lose her mind with their antics.

-all three kids sleeping in the same bed on Christmas Eve, waking up at 4 am and trying to negotiate unwrapping presents.

After Maddie left us, some of the proudest moments happened when people I didn't know came up to me. They shared stories about Maddie, saying how she helped strangers, stood up to bullies for people she didn't know, and made others feel special. Many told me she was super kind and had a way of making them feel heard.

But now, as time goes by, some of these stories are starting to fade. I don't want that to happen. Pictures and videos help, but I need to keep Maddie's memory alive in my mind. She'll always have a place in my heart, but those special stories about Maddie's personality need to be remembered. Writing this book has been a way for me to bring those stories back.

So much has been said about Maddie after she passed away, but I want to remember her for the person she was and the wonderful life she lived.

Chapter 33: Embracing Resilience: Illuminating Paths Beyond the Shadows

In the labyrinth of adolescence, where emotions swirl like a tempest and uncertainties cast shadows on the path ahead, it's imperative for both parents and teens to acknowledge a stark reality—the spectre of suicide. The journey recounted in these pages unfolds against the backdrop of a society grappling with an alarming rise in mental health challenges among its youth. The narrative is woven with threads of grief, resilience, and the enduring bonds of family.

The prevalence of teenage struggles, often concealed behind smiles and social media posts, underscores the importance of confronting the uncomfortable truths about mental health. Suicide, once a distant concept, has become an unsettling reality in the lives of many families. This book serves as a beacon, urging readers to navigate beyond the veil of naivety and confront the profound impact that mental health can have on young minds.

It is a poignant reminder that amidst the shadows of despair, there exists a multitude of stories where resilience triumphs over darkness. The journey through adolescence, with all its pitfalls and peaks, is navigable. The narratives shared here illuminate the path of those who faced the abyss and emerged stronger on the other side. These are stories of hope, resilience, and the transformative power of love and understanding.

The societal factors contributing to the mental health crisis among teenagers cannot be overlooked. Pressures from academic expectations, the relentless scrutiny of social media, and the intricate web of relationships all play pivotal roles in shaping the emotional landscape of today's youth. As we delve into the complexities of this landscape, it becomes evident that the solution lies not in avoidance but in a steadfast commitment to understanding.

In the pursuit of answers, we must summon the courage to ask the tough questions. It's an exploration that demands honesty, vulnerability, and an unwavering commitment to fostering an environment where dialogue thrives. The pages that follow are an invitation to grapple with the uncomfortable, challenging assumptions, and dismantle the barriers that impede open conversations about mental health.

Integral to this story is the crucial role of parents in the lives of their children. Trust, that delicate bridge connecting hearts, emerges as the cornerstone of effective communication. The book underscores the necessity of cultivating an atmosphere where teens feel safe to share their struggles and triumphs. It's a call to parents to become not just guardians but confidantes, navigating the delicate balance between guidance and empowerment.

As we confront the realities of teenage mental health, it is paramount to recognize the intricate interplay of factors contributing to the struggles faced by today's youth. It is a call to action, an appeal to educators, policymakers, and society at large to actively engage in initiatives that destigmatize mental health discussions and provide accessible resources for those in need.

In the final analysis, this book is not just a recounting of personal trials; it is a collective narrative of shared experiences. It is a plea for empathy, a call to action, and an affirmation that, even in the darkest moments, there is a glimmer of hope. These stories, woven with threads of pain and healing, resilience and vulnerability, serve as a testament to the indomitable human spirit.

The journey through the teenage years is complex and fraught with challenges and uncertainties. Yet, within the complexities lies the potential for growth, understanding, and profound connection. As we turn the last page, let it be with the resolve to embrace the responsibility of fostering an environment where every teenager feels seen, heard, and valued—a world where the spectre of suicide is replaced by the triumph of resilience and the journey through adolescence is marked not by despair but by the unwavering flame of hope.

Module 7: Mental Health Resources

"The journey for urgent youth mental health assistance is a race against time, where every barrier feels like a mountain to climb, and the summit holds the promise of relief and healing."

Purpose of this Section:

Parents, in times of crisis, finding the right mental health resources for your child is crucial. We understand the challenges and want to offer support. Here's an evolving list of resources, starting in Toronto, Canada, to expand nationwide and beyond. If you have recommendations, please share them at HelpANeighbourHelpThemselves@gmail.com. Include the practitioner or service name, website, contact info, services provided, specialty, and whether they operate online or in person.

You will find the following resources available:

1. Emergency Helpline Numbers & Services:
2. Therapy and Counselling:
3. Support Groups:
4. Prevention & Self-Help Resources:

Helpline & Emergency Services will only be available within this book.

All other resources will be available through the Wake up Mental Health Resource Directory portal.

Example Entry:

- Name: Hopeful Horizons Mental Health Services
- Website: www.hopefulhorizons.ca
- Contact: Dr. Sarah Smith, sarah.smith@email.com,
- (555) 123-4567, 123 Main St, Toronto, ON
- Service: Psychologist
- Specialty: Anxiety, Depression
- Online/In Person: Both

Join our mailing list for regular updates: [Wake Up Mental Health Resource Directory Portal](www.thefinishlinegroup.com/wake-up-resource-guide)

(www.thefinishlinegroup.com/wake-up-resource-guide)

Together, let's build a comprehensive network for parents, mental health practitioners, and preventive tools. Your support and recommendations make a difference.

Thanks for making this an incredible community!

Chris

WAKE UP YOU COULD LOSE YOUR TEEN TO SUICIDE

For Teens in Crisis:

Phone 9-8-8: Mental Health Emergency Hotline (Nov.30/23)

Phone 9-1-1: Emergency Services Hotline

KidsHelpPhone.ca: Call 1-800-668-6868 or Text 686868

TalkSuicide.ca: Call 1-833-456-4566 or Text 45645

Emergency & Mental Health Facilities within Toronto:

1. **Baycrest Hospital - Clinical Services - Inpatient Unit** - 3560 Bathurst St, Toronto, ON M6A 2E1

2. **Hospital for Sick Children (The) - Mental Health Access Program (MHAP)** - 555 University Ave, Toronto, ON M5G 1X8

3. **Humber River Health - Mental Health and Addictions Program** - 1235 Wilson Ave, Toronto, ON M3M 0B2

4. **Michael Garron Hospital - Outpatient Mental Health** - 825 Coxwell Ave, Toronto, ON M4C 3E7

5. **North York General Hospital - General Site – Adult Mental Health Outpatient Services** - 4001 Leslie St, Toronto, ON M2K 1E1

6. **Scarborough Health Network - Birchmount Site – Mental Health Outpatient Program** - 3030 Birchmount Rd, Toronto, ON M1W 3W3

7. **Sinai Health System - Mount Sinai Hospital - Psychiatry - Day Treatment** - Joseph and Wolf Lebovic Health Complex, 600 University Ave, 9th Fl, Toronto, ON M5G 1X5

8. **Sunnybrook Health Sciences Centre - Adult Inpatient Unit** - 2075 Bayview Ave, Toronto, ON M4N 3M5

9. **Unity Health Toronto - St Joseph's Health Centre - Child, Adolescent and Family Mental Health** - Our Lady of Mercy, 111 Sunnyside Ave, 3rd Fl, Toronto, ON M6R 2P1

10. **University Health Network - Toronto Western Hospital - Outpatient Clinics - Mental Health (AIM)** - 399 Bathurst St, East Wing, 9th Fl, Toronto, ON M5T 2S8

11. **University Health Network - Toronto General Hospital - Clinic (Progression)** - Eaton Building, 200 Elizabeth Street, Eaton Bldg., 8th Fl, Toronto, ON M5G 2C4

12. **Women's College Hospital - Women's Mental Health Program** - 76 Grenville St, Toronto, ON M5S 1B2

13. .**Etobicoke General Hospital - Mental Health and Addiction Services - Mental Health Services for Adults - Emergency/Crisis Services** - 101 Humber College Blvd, Etobicoke, ON M9V 1R8

In the event of an Emergency dial 9-1-1 or visit a hospital emergency department near you

Get access to [Wake Up Mental Health Resource Directory Portal](#)

This directory will be updated regularly as a revised PDF. This is why we are requesting you to share your name and email.

You will be asked to subscribe so we can forward a revised copy of our ever-expanding list of resources. We hope to make this resource list available in as many major markets as possible.

Sources:

https://www.thefinishlinegroup.com/emotional-wellnessblog/toll-of-social-media-on-youth-mental-health

https://www.cdc.gov/healthyyouth/data/yrbs/pdf/YRBS_Data-Summary-Trends_Report2023_508.pdf
https://content.consultimi.com/
https://themaddieproject.ca/about-us-1

https://howareyoufeeling.org/newsmedia/2022/10/7/whatare-4-ways-we-can-build-emotional-intelligence-in-our-kids

https://howareyoufeeling.org/newsmedia/2022/8/16/illnever-accept-the-loss-of-yet-another-teen-by-suicide
https://childmind.org/article/teen-suicides-risk-factors/
https://childmind.org/article/signs-of-anxiety-in-teenagers/

https://jedfoundation.org/mental-health-and-suicidestatistics/

https://www.pbs.org/newshour/nation/suicide-amongteens-and-young-adults-reaches-highest-level-since-2000
https://www.childtrends.org/publications/teen-suicidedatabank-indicator

Copy Editor https://openai.com/

Cover and Back Cover Design by A. Abosede

WAKE UP YOU COULD LOSE YOUR TEEN TO SUICIDE

CHRIS COULTER

WAKE UP YOU COULD LOSE YOUR TEEN TO SUICIDE

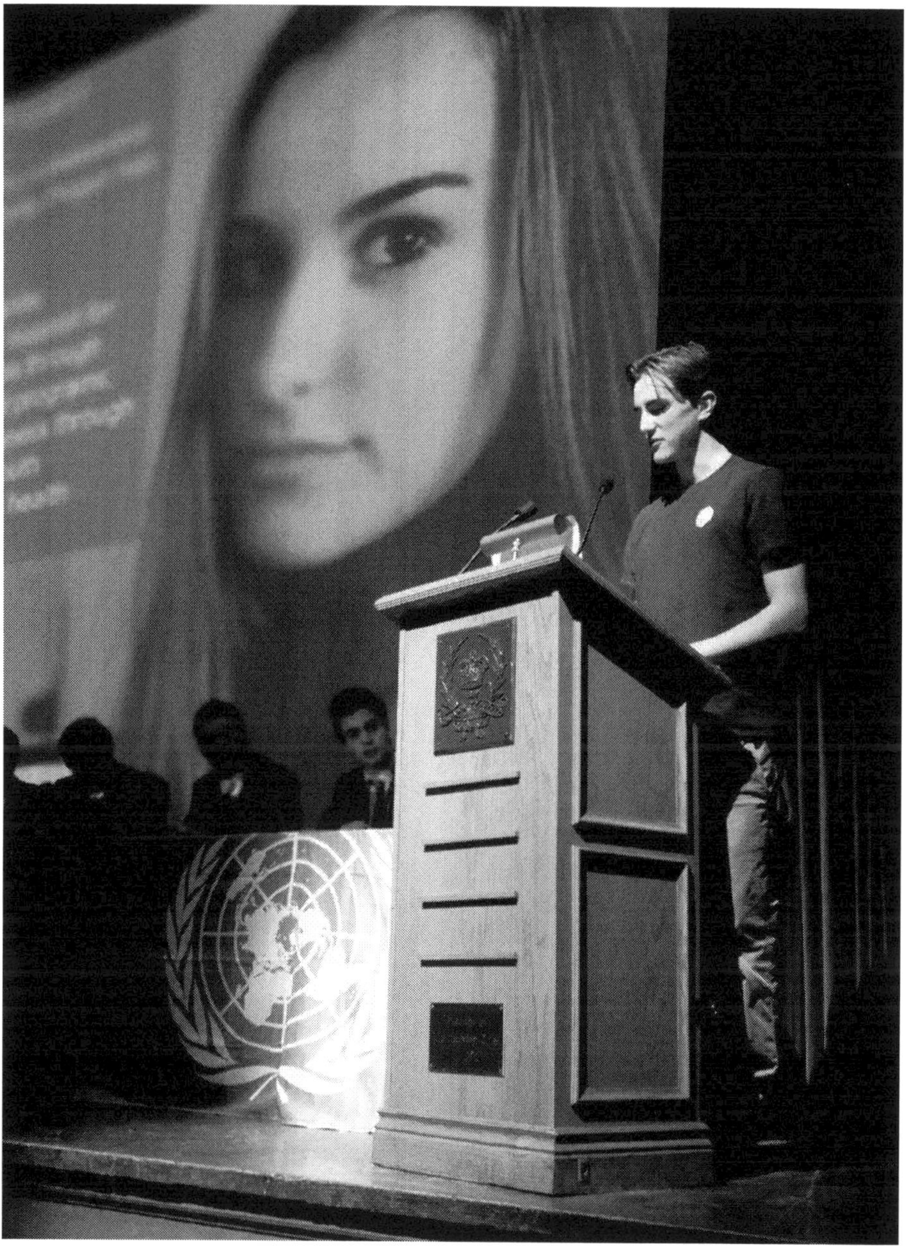

WAKE UP YOU COULD LOSE YOUR TEEN TO SUICIDE

CHRIS COULTER

WAKE UP YOU COULD LOSE YOUR TEEN TO SUICIDE

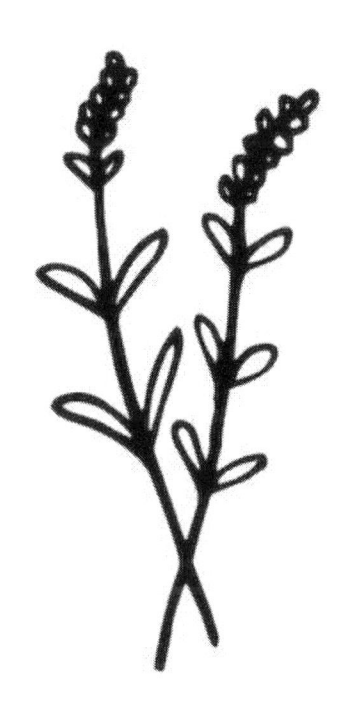